Living LITERATURE

READING PROSE

Barbara Marshall

Hodder & Stoughton

A MEMBER OF THE HODDER HEADLINE GROUP

Acknowledgements

Thanks to: the students at Varndean college who tried out the activities and contributed to this book, particularly to Vanessa for her diagrams.

For Chris, John and Stevie

The publishers would like to thank the following for their kind permission to reproduce copyright material:

p. 3, extracts from *The Age of Lead* by Margaret Atwood, 1991; *Icemen: A History of the Arctic and its Explorers* by Conefrey and Jordan, 1998; Blackwood's Edinburgh Magazine, November 1855; *Frankenstein* by Mary Shelley, 1818; *The Voyage of the Narwah* by Andrea Barratt, 2000; p. 13, title pages from *Oroonoko* by Aphra Behn; *Moll Flanders* by Daniel Defoe; *Robinson Crusoe* by Daniel Defoe; *Pamela* by Samuel Richardson; *Mansfield Park* by Jane Austen; *The Mysteries of Udolpho* by Ann Radcliffe, all Penguin Books Ltd; p. 16 Contents Page extracted from *House of Leaves* by Mark Z. Danielewski, © Mark Z. Danielewski, published by Transworld Publishers, a division of The Random House Group Ltd. All rights reserved.; p. 17, from *An Introduction to the English Novel* by Arnold Kettle; p. 19, from *The Great Tradition* by F R Leavis, 1948; pp. 19–20, from *An Introduction to Women's Writing* by Lyn Pykett, 1998; pp. 30–31, from *The Longest Memory* by Fred D'Aguiar; published by Chatto & Windus/Vintage. Reprinted by permission of The Random House Group Ltd. p. 34, from *Wuthering Heights* by Emily Brontë, 1847; pp. 35–36, Reading Group Guide for *Beloved* by Toni Morrison. Reprinted by permission of International Creative Management, Inc. © Toni Morrison; p. 37, extracts from *Down Among the Women* by Fay Weldon, 1973, Penguin Books; *Harry Potter and the Chamber of Secrets* by J K Rowling, 1999; pp. 38–39, *Solo Dance* by Jayne Anne Phillips, Faber & Faber, 1993; pp. 45, 46, 47, 48, extracts from *Emma* by Jane Austen; p. 57, from *Frankenstein* by Mary Shelley, 1818; pp. 58–60, *The Smell* by Patrick McGrath, © 1991, reproduced by permission of the author, care of Rogers, Coleridge & White Ltd, 20 Powis Mews, London W11 1JN; p. 63, from *Jane Eyre* by Charlotte Brontë; 1847; pp. 63–64, from *Great Expectations* by Charles Dickens, 1861; p. 64, from *A Portrait of the Artist as a Young Man*, by James Joyce, 1916; pp. 65–70, *The Man Without a Temperament* by Katherine Mansfield, 1920; pp. 74–75, from the essay, *Modern Fiction* by Virginia Woolf, 1919; p. 78, from *The Bloody Chamber* by Angela Carter, Vintage, 1995; p. 79, *Blue-Bearded Lover* by Joyce Carol Oates, The Ecco Press, 1988; pp. 81–87, *Dreaming Diana: Twelve Frames* by Alison MacLeod, 2001.

Every effort has been made to trace copyright holders of material reproduced in this book. Any rights not acknowledged will be acknowledged in subsequent printings if notice is given to the publisher.

Order queries: please contact Bookpoint Ltd, 130 Milton Park, Abingdon, Oxon OX14 4SB. Telephone: (44) 01235 827720, Fax: (44) 01235 400454. Lines are open from 9.00–6.00pm, Monday to Saturday, with a 24 hour message answering service. Email address: orders@bookpoint.co.uk

British Library Cataloguing in Publication Data
A catalogue entry for this title is available from The British Library

ISBN 0 340 79955 2

Published by Hodder & Stoughton Educational Scotland
First published 2001
Impression number   10 9 8 7 6 5 4 3 2 1
Year   2007 2006 2005 2004 2003 2002 2001

Cover photo from The Ronald Grant Archive
Typeset by Fakenham Photosetting Limited, Fakenham, Norfolk
Printed in Great Britain for Hodder & Stoughton Educational, a division of Hodder Headline Plc, 338 Euston Road, London NW1 3BH by J. W. Arrowsmith Ltd, Bristol

Contents

INTRODUCTION

This book is designed for students taking English Literature at Advanced level. You are required to study prose texts and the vast majority of those prose texts are novels by English, or English speaking writers. The new specifications for AS and A level have given much greater emphasis to genre, the type of text and the conventions it works with, and to relationships between texts. It is also now essential to have an understanding of contexts and different critical interpretations. This book is concerned with placing your study of prose in that light. Studying for your A level you will need, therefore, to consider not only the texts specified by your examination board, but wider issues that take you out from that text to other texts and other readers. This book invites you to think about what kind of text a novel or prose fiction is, why and how it developed and how it has been regarded. Some popular examination choices are discussed as examples, as well as some unfamiliar texts, but the idea is that you will be able to apply what you learn and the many questions raised about prose to the texts you have been given to study.

The first section of the book is designed to give you some frameworks for examining prose texts and addresses questions about genre and contexts. The second section of the book develops your understanding of contexts, concepts and critical approaches through closer focus on texts and it moves through the early nineteenth to the early twenty-first centuries. Although each chapter is self-contained and has a particular focus, the book was conceived as a whole and you will be referred to or reminded of other sections in the book where relevant. It is designed to give you the opportunity to work on complete texts – not easy in a book on prose – so there are several short stories used that are unlikely to be familiar ones, but will raise plenty of interesting questions to apply elsewhere. The book includes a number of creative writing tasks. One of the best ways to find out what is going on when we write prose is to try it out!

Changing attitudes towards the teaching of English mean that the usefulness of distinctions between fiction and non-fiction have been much debated. Clearly there are very interesting relationships between texts such as biographies or travel writing for example, and fictional prose. Although this issue is touched on, it would need a longer book to do justice to non-fiction texts which need proper historicising and contextualising too, for which there has simply not been enough space. Given that most specifications concentrate on fiction, that is what this book does. Many of the tasks could equally be applied to non-fiction texts.

The last sections of the book offer advice on writing about prose, using critical terminology and further reading. The assessment objectives are included here and these are referred to throughout the book. Activities which could be used for key skills are marked in the text. Throughout the book key terms are explained in context and put in **boldface** if they are also defined in the glossary.

Finally, the activities in this book are often followed by a commentary. You should consider the ideas raised in the commentaries before moving on in the chapters: the sequence is intended to develop your thinking. It may be very tempting to read the commentary rather than undertake the activity, but you will not learn effectively this way.

1

What is Prose?

Prose: not poetry, not drama, prose

In this introductory chapter you will start to think about the ways we define and use terms like *prose* and the *novel*. As students of this subject, English Literature, you have probably already asked the question, 'What is Literature?' You have probably realised that this is not an easy question to answer, finding that it might depend on who you are, where you are, and when you are! If 'literature' is a shifting category open to question and revision and shaped by context, then within that, 'prose' is perhaps the most open sub-category of all within literature. Drama and poetry texts declare themselves to be 'literary' as soon as we look at them on the page or hear them spoken or see them performed on a stage.

ACTIVITY 1

Think about the following:

A
*Is what you
are reading
        now
a poem
    or

not?*

B
Is what you are reading now prose or not?

COMMENTARY

A is an interesting question, which invites discussion but **B** is a bit of a problem. It's really not a very exciting idea to debate. We recognise poems, for example, by their 'otherness' but prose seems to be straightforward and familiar. The word processor was not at all happy with **A** and wanted to correct its punctuation and layout: **B** was just what it expected. The word 'prosaic' is used to indicate something rather boring and leaden; in the Collins English Dictionary, one of the definitions of prose is 'commonplace or dull'; another is 'in ordinary usage'. Prose is of course what we use all the time as speakers and writers. As a student on a course in English Literature you will be required to study prose, but hopefully you will not be approaching the course expecting this to be the dull bit, with texts selected for their exemplary and magnificent dullness. You probably expect prose to have a different meaning in this context, that you will study a particular kind of 'prose' and that you will study it in particular kinds of ways and be stimulated by it. In this chapter you will start to examine the way that prose is regarded in the **discourse** of English Literature (the ways we think, talk and write about literature as an academic subject) and also what we understand by the idea of 'reading'.

What sorts of prose might be read as literature?

Perhaps the most straightforward answer to this question would be the sorts of prose texts that are set on English Literature courses.

ACTIVITY 2

- First, talk about and note down the sorts of prose texts you enjoy reading and say why you read them.
- Then find out about the prose texts set for A level examinations. You can do this by looking at examination specifications or examination papers which are published and also available on the Boards' websites. You can ask your teachers. You could find out about the texts set by your own Examination Board or you could find out what the other Boards are offering too.
- How many of the texts have you heard of or read?
- Are they fiction or non-fiction?
- Do they belong to any particular type or genre of text – for example, romance, crime or science fiction?
- Why do you think they have been chosen?
- What do you expect to study in them?

COMMENTARY

A questionnaire for A level students including some of these questions revealed that many of them gave very different answers to why they read novels and why novels were studied in English Literature. They *read* novels, they wrote, 'to be entertained'; for 'escapism'; for 'relaxation'. On the other hand, they *studied* novels 'to explore the human condition'; 'to appreciate the writer's use of language and form'; 'to improve our understanding of human relations'; 'because they can be understood on a number of different levels'. There was considerable agreement not only about what they were doing, but also about the kind of text they expected to study. Perhaps unsurprisingly, they were already a 'community' of readers. Despite coming to the college from different schools, they constituted an 'interpretative' community who shared similar ideas about prose texts. Later in this book we will return to consider where this consensus of views might come from and how it might be significant in the ways we read texts.

Fiction and non-fiction

The students who completed the survey expected to study 'fiction' for the prose texts on an examination course. It is interesting that the dictionary definition for 'fiction' sounds almost opposite to the 'dull' definition of prose; instead it is described as 'inventive' or 'imaginative' writing. This brings along with it another category we find ourselves using: 'non-fiction'. Non-fiction is likely to be prose that is not inventive, but still has 'literary' qualities – journals or travel writing for example. If we can study both as literature, then is it possible to distinguish between them and identify what features they might share? Clearly these terms start to throw up more questions than answers. For example, is non-fiction always 'true'?

Read the following brief extracts from fiction and non-fiction texts. They are all concerned with explorers who tried to find a way to cross the Arctic to the North Pole in the nineteenth century.

As you read the passages, consider what sort of text you think each extract comes from. Note, as you go, the clues that prompted your thoughts and where your views change or develop.

Then, in small groups, discuss your notes. Try to identify the factors that influenced your views, such as the vocabulary, the sentence structure, the use of descriptive or **figurative** language, the voice or narrator in the text.

Two of the extracts were written in the nineteenth century; the others were written recently. Can you tell which were written when? How?

1 'The man has been buried for a hundred and fifty years. They dug a hole in the frozen gravel, deep into the permafrost, and put him down there so the wolves wouldn't get to him. Or that is the speculation.
When they dug the hole the permafrost was exposed to the air, which was warmer. This made the permafrost melt. But it froze again after the man was covered up, so that when he was brought to the surface he was completely enclosed in ice. They took the lid off the coffin and it was like those maraschino cherries you used to freeze in ice-cube trays for fancy tropical drinks: a vague shape, looming through a solid cloud.'

2 'Franklin had now been gone for more than four years. With the failure of the relief expeditions, anxiety reached fever pitch. To the newspaper reading public it was a sensational mystery: how could two ships 'fitted and strengthened by every process of ingenuity, to meet and overcome every obstacle' simply vanish? What kind of place is the Arctic, which can swallow up the 'elite of maritime England' without leaving a trace?

3 No; there are no more sunny continents – no more islands of the blessed – hidden under the far horizon, tempting the dreamer over the undiscovered sea; nothing but those weird and tragic shores, whose cliffs of everlasting ice and mainlands of frozen snow, which have never produced anything to us but a late and sad discovery of depths of human heroism, patience and bravery, such as imagination could scarcely dream of.

4 'I try in vain to be persuaded that the pole is the seat of frost and desolation; it ever presents itself to my imagination as the region of beauty and delight. There, Margaret, the sun is for ever visible; its broad disk just skirting the horizon, and diffusing a perpetual splendour. There – for with your leave, my sister, I will put some trust in preceding navigators – there snow and frost are banished; and sailing over a calm sea, we may be wafted to a land surpassing in wonders and beauty every region hitherto discovered on the habitable globe.'

5 Somewhere in those icy waters, Franklin and his men might still be trapped in the Erebus and the Terror. Even if they couldn't be found, many new species, even new lands, were there to be discovered. Erasmus thought of being free, this time, to investigate everything without the noxious Navy discipline. He thought of northern sights to parallel, even exceed, his brief experience in the Antarctic; of discoveries in natural history that might prove extraordinarily important. Then he thought of his sister, who appeared on the porch with her white dress foaming like a spray of catalpa blossom.
'You should go in,' she said to Zeke. 'All the guests are longing to talk to with you.'
He leapt up the steps and she steered him inside. With a swirl of skirts she turned to Erasmus.
'Will you go?' she said.

COMMENTARY All the texts apart from number four are based on an historical event. This was when Sir John Franklin's expedition to the Arctic ended in tragedy and all the men were untraced until some bodies preserved by the ice were found 100 years later. This is a true history but also a fabulous story, with elements of romance, adventure, mystery and detection as well as vast descriptive and metaphorical possibilities: the 'journey' has been a key idea for novelists since the early days of the novel in the eighteenth century. Why do you think this might be?

1 We realise that this has been written much later than the event because it talks about the excavation of the body and it uses a very modern simile, *'like those maraschino cherries you used to freeze in ice-cube trays'*. This gives the writing a self-conscious and literary quality, although it also uses the language of explication, which sounds precise and scientific (*'the permafrost was exposed to the air ...'*). The reader feels they are being directly addressed by this passage, in a way that is both remote and authoritative (*'Or that is the speculation'*) and familiar and friendly (*'you used to freeze ...'*). It is a mixture of voices and styles, sounding both 'factual' and 'fictional'. This first extract is taken from a late twentieth century short story, *The Age of Lead*, by Margaret Atwood (1991), which opens with the narrator watching a documentary about the bodies of the 'icemen'.

2 The second passage also uses figurative language that perhaps sounds familiar and contemporary (*'reached fever pitch ... can swallow up ...'*). It excites the reader's curiosity with its use of rhetorical questions and the voice in the text sounds informed and depersonalised (*'With the failure of the relief expeditions, anxiety reached fever pitch'*). This was taken from a history text, but the original was intended for a television audience, which perhaps gives it this distinctive style. Extract from *Icemen: A History of the Arctic and its Explorers* by Conefrey and Jordan (1998).

3 This has a very elegiac or sad tone with its repetition of negatives and its mournful imagery. The length of the sentence and its epic, even religious language (*'islands of the blessed'*) perhaps suggest this is not a recent text. Its embellished style and direct address to the reader may give it a literary feel (*'No; there are no more sunny continents ... nothing but those weird and tragic shores'*). This is a piece of nineteenth century journalism, responding to the loss of the Franklin expedition and was published in Blackwood's Edinburgh Magazine in November, 1855.

4 The hyperbole (extravagant) and romantic language of this description of the Arctic sounds extremely similar to that of extract three. This text seems to be addressing a particular person, Margaret, and sounds like a letter. It comes from the opening sequence of Mary Shelley's nineteenth century novel, *Frankenstein* (1818), set in the Arctic where Frankenstein is pursuing his hideous creation to the ends of the world. Using the letter form, which we shall return to later in this book, may give a sense of authenticity, of a 'true' event.

5 This extract is from a recently published novel, *The Voyage of the Narwhal* (2000) by Andrea Barratt, which uses the historical material of the Franklin expedition to create a fictional search. As in extract four,

the reader is positioned inside the thoughts of a character. It mixes empirical (provable, not abstract) references to historical events, the Erebus and the Terror, with the language of romantic fiction: '*With a swirl of skirts she turned . . .*'. The use of dialogue is a technique we tend to associate with fiction.

These extracts seem to have a very hybrid nature with a number of different sorts of voice at work in them. This activity makes us think about the difficulties involved in seeing texts as categories; the relationships between fiction and non-fiction texts are hard to distinguish and they are also subject to changing values and attitudes. English Literature as an academic subject explicitly values fiction; English Language or History, for example, would value non-fiction as part of their course requirements. Cultural beliefs and views on learning do not stand still and the late twentieth century has seen developments in subjects such as English and History that debate the slipperiness or even collapse, of fixed categories such as fact or fiction. The words history and story come from the same Latin root and in previous centuries have been used interchangeably. Some of the early novels of the eighteenth century called their invented stories of characters 'histories'. In much more recent decades, novelists have frequently imported 'historical' events or characters into 'fiction' as a way of opening up questions about the validity of either category, history or fiction, as a way of 'knowing' the world. It would be possible and extremely interesting to apply the approaches in this book, such as understanding the contexts of the reading and writing of the text, to non-fiction texts and some of you may have the opportunity to do this by examining autobiographies or travel writing, for example, as part of your course. However, this book concentrates upon the novel, since this is where the emphasis lies at A level.

This activity is designed to make you analyse your expectations of fiction as a genre and also to start you thinking about the critical approaches that you use. Of course, what you did not have at first were any *contexts*, such as what sort of text is this (**genre** and **form**); when was it written, in what society, and by whom. You were expected to find things to say about the '*literariness*' of the text, which may well be something you feel quite comfortable doing or certainly expect to do. That is to say, this practice of '*close reading*' (paying attention to language) is characteristic of much English teaching. It is very important to be able to develop detailed analytical reading in order to meet the examination's assessment objectives, but there are other critical approaches of equal interest, that we will explore later.

'Narrative . . . is simply there, like life itself . . .'

(Roland Barthes, *Introduction to The Structural Analysis of Narrative*)

One of the reasons why it seems false to separate history and fiction is because they both rely on **narrative**, the unfolding of events. In fact, a lot of communication depends on narrative.

In pairs, try the following two, quick activities. You should try to work with someone you do not know well.

1 Tell your partner about yourself. Your partner should jot down notes on what you say. Reverse roles and repeat the task.

2 Think about something that happened yesterday – it doesn't have to be unusual or exciting; a visit to a friend, a journey to school or college, what happened in a lesson, a night out. Tell your partner about it, *without using words.*

What happened when you tried this?

In talking about yourself, where did you start? Did you follow a sequence? What information did you select as saying something about yourself? Why? When you were 'telling without words', did you use mime? Sketches? Did they follow a sequence, like a storyboard?

This brief task may well have revealed that we often use narrative techniques, such as setting a scene, using description, following a sequence or making connections in everyday conversations. We may even try to do this where words are not available. We habitually use narrative to relate the stories of our lives; it seems to make sense of our experience. Most of us who write a diary keep it in narrative form. Stories are all around us, from the television news to written instructions on how to access the internet. Some would argue that narrative is fundamental to the way we think and that from an early age babies and children demand and respond to it – 'Tell me a story', 'What happened next? In the end?'

Consider, for example, the way narrative is frequently used to deliver a recipe. Information that could be given in lists or diagrams is instead part of a story, like this extract from a recent cookery book on tart recipes: *'Scattered with sugar, dotted with butter, it was cooked for ten minutes before I poured a layer of peach jam, melted with a bit of water, but not sieved, over the fruit, returning it to the oven for 10 minutes. We ate the sugary slices in our hands, crisply crusted edges, slightly sogged middles, with their thickened purply juices bleeding into the apple edges'.* With its use of first person narration, narrative sequence, rich descriptive vocabulary and lyrical style, this sounds as though it could come from a novel.

The ubiquity (presence all around us) and flexibility of narrative, in a way, makes the task of a book like this harder. If narrative is everywhere then it feels not only familiar but natural. As a student of English Literature you know that you will consider not only what a text says, but how it says it, how it has been constructed. This can be a lot harder to do when the way of saying it seems natural.

'Her life is just like a novel'

However much we might see our lives as narratives, we do tend to distinguish between 'life' and a novel. This will be discussed much more fully later on. For a start, we tend to have a clear idea in our mind about what a novel is.

ACTIVITY 5

First write your own definition of the term 'a novel'. Then look up as many definitions as you can of the term 'novel'. Use dictionaries, encyclopaedia, guidebooks or reference texts on Literature. Try to find a range of sources, preferably also written at different times in history. Then, with a partner, underline or list the key terms you find in each explanation.

What do you find? Is there agreement? Do there seem to be any vague or disputed issues? Do the definitions explain the term through what it is not? Or through a history of the form? Formulate some questions about the novel that you would find interesting to pursue as you read further.

This is the Oxford English Dictionary's definition of a novel. Are there any parts of it you would like to dispute?

'A fictitious prose narrative or tale of considerable length (now usually one long enough to fill one or more volumes) in which characters and actions representative of the real life of past or present times are portrayed in a plot of more or less complexity.'

We have already seen that the term 'fictitious' or 'fiction' is open to debate. This definition then goes on to prioritise characters, plot and the representation of 'real life of past or present times'. Later in this book we will consider whether this defines a particular type of novel which has been the dominant one in the subject of English Literature. For the moment, you might like to consider whether or not this satisfactorily describes all the novels you have experienced reading.

If you were able to use an historical dictionary, you would have found that the term 'the novel' does not enter English vocabulary until quite late, becoming established in the eighteenth century. Until then, the word *novel* as a noun, rather than an adjective meaning new or fresh, meant 'news'. We would certainly be surprised to switch on to 'The Ten O'Clock Novels' rather than News, although we still talk of news stories. Again, this suggests an interesting relationship between 'true' stories and 'invented' ones and in Chapter 2 we will look more closely at the origins of the novel.

This chapter has introduced you to some key questions involved in studying prose texts. You have thought about what we mean when we use the term prose and the complexities surrounding the labels or categories we put writing into. You have started to think about the key concept of narrative and the form in which we most commonly encounter it on A level courses – the novel.

2 The Story of the Novel

At the end of the first chapter we started to think about when the term, the novel, came into popular use. In this chapter we will look in a bit more detail at the history of the novel. Novels do not come just from the writer's desire to tell a story. If you had never read a novel, it would be extremely difficult to write one, or one that would be accepted by the rest of us as being a novel. Questions about **genre** (what is the nature of this text), *context* (where did it come from) and *interpretation* (how can we read it) which you deal with at A level, need to be informed by an understanding of how the novel has developed in history and how attitudes of writers and readers towards this type of text have shaped it. It may seem an old-fashioned approach to ask you to consider this, an approach more akin to the way Literature was studied at the beginning of the twentieth century, rather than at the beginning of the twenty-first, but there is no easy answer to such large questions, nor is there only one history of the novel. Rather, there have been a number of different stories told about the novel, all of which raise interesting questions for us about when and why the form became popular, who wrote it and who read it. This chapter is therefore quite a challenging one. There is quite a lot of information to take in and think about. You may wish to return to this chapter when you have established confidence in working with prose, or when you feel secure in your understanding of your set texts and would like to be able to contextualise them. The timeline in this chapter is designed so that you can refer back to it to contextualise other texts you encounter, either in this book or as set texts.

The development of novels

When Henry Fielding wrote the Preface to his novel *Joseph Andrews* in 1742, he claimed, '... *it may not be improper to premise a few words concerning this kind of writing, which I do not remember to have seen hitherto attempted in our language.*' Most literary histories trace the origins of the novel to the early eighteenth century. In comparison with poetry and drama it is therefore quite a young form of writing. The word 'novel' means new. This is often quite surprising to students, for whom the novel is generally the most familiar of the three main genres. So where did it come from and why did this so-called new form arrive? In order to consider this, we need to look at these 'novel' texts themselves and at what was going on around them, that is, the circumstances that produced them.

ACTIVITY 6

In a pair or a small group, look carefully at the timeline below. For the purposes of this first activity, look particularly closely at the sections on the 1700s and 1800s. Discuss the events and developments of the period given here and in your group draw up a number of possible reasons why the novel might have risen to popularity in this time.

You could use the following prompts to gather ideas:

- Who are the readers?
- How easy are books to get hold of?
- What is the importance of women as writers and readers?
- What changing ideas and social and economic developments might be significant for readers, writers and publishers?
- Women readers/writers
- Social and economic change.

COMMENTARY

Obviously, the material included on the timeline is very selective. It would be a good idea to extend your knowledge by using reference books, CD ROMs or on-line searches. An understanding of contexts is one of the assessment objectives at AS level and evaluation of their significance is assessed at A2 level. When you study your set texts, you will need a specific and detailed contextual picture. We shall examine how you might approach this more closely in Chapter 6. Here, however, we are looking very broadly at the ways in which social, economic, manufacturing and philosophical development over decades and centuries may have influenced the increasing publication and reading of novels.

Growing literacy is clearly an important factor. The novel is privately consumed so, unlike stage drama or oral poetry, it requires an audience who can read. It also has a material existence as a printed text rather than as a performance, so it needs to be printed and purchased. As the industrial revolution developed, and technological and transportation changes made printing quicker and cheaper, more novels could be produced. In the eighteenth and nineteenth centuries, they were still very expensive, as you can see from the timeline, so only the upper classes could afford them. The development of circulating libraries widened access to novels, now increasingly published in several volumes: 'three-deckers'. Although this was still really only affordable by the middle-classes, the popular chapbooks of the eighteenth century (cheap pamphlets that might feature ballads, stories or potted novels), cheaper reprints and the growing market for newspapers and magazines in the nineteenth century contributed to the sense of a growing readership. However, it was not until the twentieth century that state education and paperback production made the novel widely accessible.

Other critics have pointed to social and economic developments as generating a new kind of writing and we shall look at this more closely later in this chapter. Both economic theory (for example, free trade and capital enterprise) and influential philosophers and political writers were emphasising the cultivation of the individual, so individual 'histories' or stories of development were popular. Such novels are sometimes called **Bildungsroman**, meaning 'education or formation novel', usually from childhood. Individual and democratic rights were being asserted through radical political movements and changing social class relationships,

POLITICAL EVENTS – NATIONAL AND INTERNATIONAL

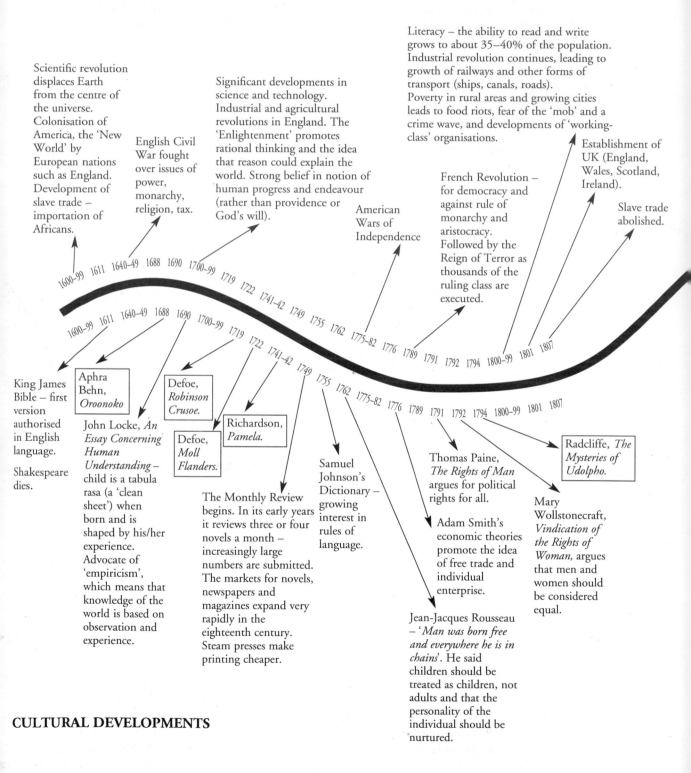

Scientific revolution displaces Earth from the centre of the universe. Colonisation of America, the 'New World' by European nations such as England. Development of slave trade – importation of Africans.

English Civil War fought over issues of power, monarchy, religion, tax.

Significant developments in science and technology. Industrial and agricultural revolutions in England. The 'Enlightenment' promotes rational thinking and the idea that reason could explain the world. Strong belief in notion of human progress and endeavour (rather than providence or God's will).

Literacy – the ability to read and write grows to about 35–40% of the population. Industrial revolution continues, leading to growth of railways and other forms of transport (ships, canals, roads). Poverty in rural areas and growing cities leads to food riots, fear of the 'mob' and a crime wave, and developments of 'working-class' organisations.

American Wars of Independence

French Revolution – for democracy and against rule of monarchy and aristocracy. Followed by the Reign of Terror as thousands of the ruling class are executed.

Establishment of UK (England, Wales, Scotland, Ireland).

Slave trade abolished.

1600–99 1611 1640–49 1688 1690 1700–99 1719 1722 1741–42 1749 1755 1762 1775–82 1776 1789 1791 1792 1794 1800–99 1801 1807

King James Bible – first version authorised in English language.

Shakespeare dies.

Aphra Behn, *Oroonoko*

John Locke, *An Essay Concerning Human Understanding* – child is a tabula rasa (a 'clean sheet') when born and is shaped by his/her experience. Advocate of 'empiricism', which means that knowledge of the world is based on observation and experience.

Defoe, *Robinson Crusoe.*

Defoe, *Moll Flanders.*

Richardson, *Pamela.*

The Monthly Review begins. In its early years it reviews three or four novels a month – increasingly large numbers are submitted. The markets for novels, newspapers and magazines expand very rapidly in the eighteenth century. Steam presses make printing cheaper.

Samuel Johnson's Dictionary – growing interest in rules of language.

Jean-Jacques Rousseau – '*Man was born free and everywhere he is in chains*'. He said children should be treated as children, not adults and that the personality of the individual should be nurtured.

Thomas Paine, *The Rights of Man* argues for political rights for all.

Adam Smith's economic theories promote the idea of free trade and individual enterprise.

Mary Wollstonecraft, *Vindication of the Rights of Woman*, argues that men and women should be considered equal.

Radcliffe, *The Mysteries of Udolpho.*

CULTURAL DEVELOPMENTS

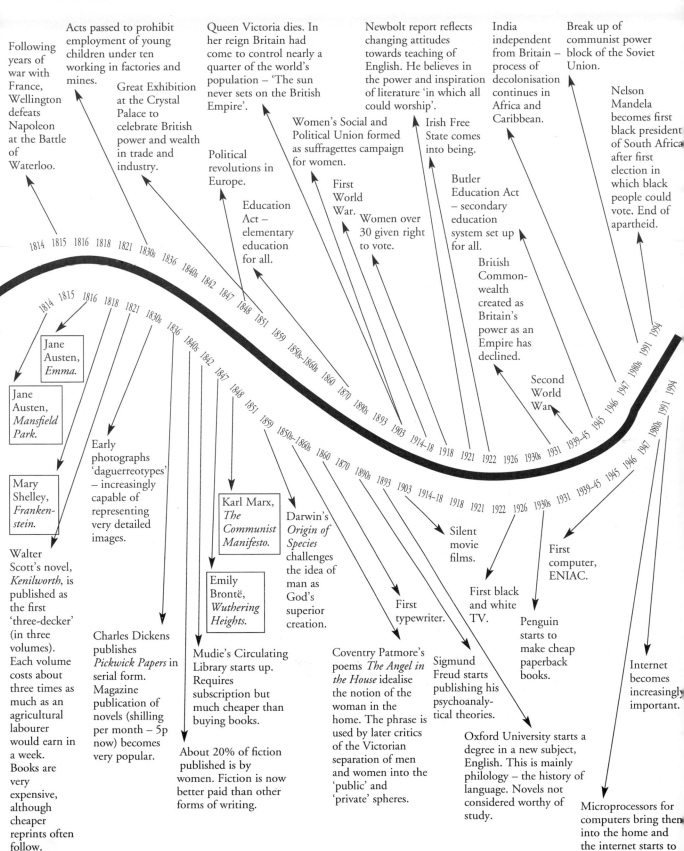

Following years of war with France, Wellington defeats Napoleon at the Battle of Waterloo.

Acts passed to prohibit employment of young children under ten working in factories and mines.

Great Exhibition at the Crystal Palace to celebrate British power and wealth in trade and industry.

Queen Victoria dies. In her reign Britain had come to control nearly a quarter of the world's population – 'The sun never sets on the British Empire'.

Political revolutions in Europe.

Education Act – elementary education for all.

Women's Social and Political Union formed as suffragettes campaign for women.

First World War.

Women over 30 given right to vote.

Newbolt report reflects changing attitudes towards teaching of English. He believes in the power and inspiration of literature 'in which all could worship'.

Irish Free State comes into being.

India independent from Britain – process of decolonisation continues in Africa and Caribbean.

Butler Education Act – secondary education system set up for all.

British Common-wealth created as Britain's power as an Empire has declined.

Break up of communist power block of the Soviet Union.

Nelson Mandela becomes first black president of South Africa after first election in which black people could vote. End of apartheid.

Second World War.

1814　1815　1816　1818　1821　1830s　1836　1840s　1842　1847　1848　1851　1859　1850s–1860s　1860　1870　1890s　1893　1903　1914–18　1918　1921　1922　1926　1930s　1931　1939–45　1945　1946　1947　1980s　1991　1994

1814　1815　1816　1818　1821　1830s　1836　1840s　1842　1847　1848　1851　1859　1850s–1860s　1860　1870　1890s　1893　1903　1914–18　1918　1921　1922　1926　1930s　1931　1939–45　1945　1946　1947　1980s　1991　1994

Jane Austen, *Emma*.

Jane Austen, *Mansfield Park*.

Mary Shelley, *Franken-stein*.

Walter Scott's novel, *Kenilworth*, is published as the first 'three-decker' (in three volumes). Each volume costs about three times as much as an agricultural labourer would earn in a week. Books are very expensive, although cheaper reprints often follow.

Early photographs 'daguerreotypes' – increasingly capable of representing very detailed images.

Charles Dickens publishes *Pickwick Papers* in serial form. Magazine publication of novels (shilling per month – 5p now) becomes very popular.

Karl Marx, *The Communist Manifesto*.

Emily Brontë, *Wuthering Heights*.

Mudie's Circulating Library starts up. Requires subscription but much cheaper than buying books.

About 20% of fiction published is by women. Fiction is now better paid than other forms of writing.

Darwin's *Origin of Species* challenges the idea of man as God's superior creation.

First typewriter.

Coventry Patmore's poems *The Angel in the House* idealise the notion of the woman in the home. The phrase is used by later critics of the Victorian separation of men and women into the 'public' and 'private' spheres.

Silent movie films.

First black and white TV.

Sigmund Freud starts publishing his psychoanaly-tical theories.

Oxford University starts a degree in a new subject, English. This is mainly philology – the history of language. Novels not considered worthy of study.

First computer, ENIAC.

Penguin starts to make cheap paperback books.

Internet becomes increasingly important.

Microprocessors for computers bring them into the home and the internet starts to develop.

including debates on the position of women. Although the first phase of the English women's movement was not until the end of the nineteenth century and the second phase – what we would now call feminism – did not occur until the 1960s, back in the 1790s Mary Wollstonecraft and others were already arguing for women's rights. Women as writers and as readers were heavily involved in debates about the novel from the eighteenth century onwards. It has been argued that women were more likely to write prose fiction than poetry or drama because novels could be written in, and about, the 'private sphere', the domestic world that the ideologies of the eighteenth and nineteenth centuries expected women to be confined to. When Charlotte Brontë wrote to the Poet Laureate of her day, Robert Southey, about her desire to write, she was firmly told: 'Literature cannot be the business of a woman's life, and it ought not to be'. However, as a new and developing form, the novel was exciting and less exclusive than the traditionally male-dominated genre of poetry, which seemed to demand a 'classical' education, denied to girls; and it did not require engagement in the public world of theatre. It remains significant, however, that women such as the Brontës published under pseudonyms, and others, such as Mary Shelley with *Frankenstein*, first published their works anonymously.

Think again about what you have discussed in this activity. Remember that an understanding of contexts will be part of your study of the set texts. Talk in pairs about a pre-twentieth century text that you know well. Note down your ideas about the ways such historical information affects your reading and understanding of older texts.

Examining early novels

In order to examine some of these ideas further, we need to look at a more limited chunk of time and at some specific examples. Old texts looked quite different from the products of today's publishing industry. If you study a Jane Austen novel, you will study it in a repackaged modern paperback format. If we look at the original texts, however, it is easier to see the books as products of their time rather than as part of our twenty-first century reading experience. They do not look familiar and we can ask questions about the way they were originally presented to their readers.

ACTIVITY 7

The following are title pages of some early novels.
In small groups, talk about the information and the wording given on these title pages.
What does this suggest to your group about:

- the content of the texts
- the reader's expectations of such texts
- the attitudes to the writing and writers of these texts?

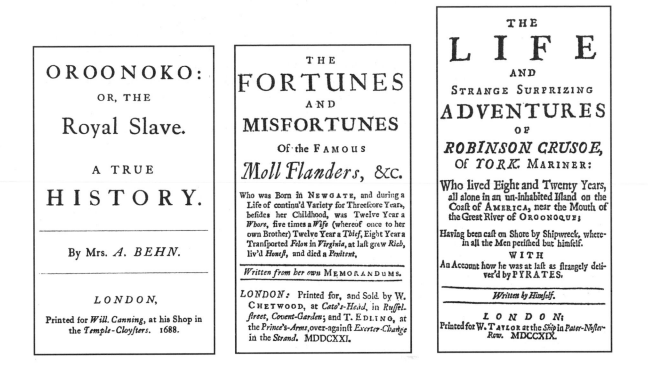

Title pages of some early novels

COMMENTARY   *Oroonoko's* title page is interesting for a number of reasons; firstly due to its date; of 1688. Until recently, many commentators on the novel claimed that it 'started' in the next century, the early 1700s. However, critics interested in women's writing have researched and retrieved less well-known writings by women and there has been extensive scholarship in such areas, putting other writers into the **canon**; which refers to the texts considered important in Literature studies. You will have noted that the book was written by Mrs A. Behn. This also counters the commonly held belief that women usually had to publish as men, using male pseudonyms like the Brontë sisters or 'George' Eliot. Aphra Behn was well known in her time for her plays and poetry, as well as prose pieces like *Oroonoko*. Interest in her work has been revived and is increasingly set on the curriculum in Higher Education and A level. You may have been surprised that the subject of the book was slavery, which might seem a very modern concern, with many writers today interested in the history of colonies and race relations. Behn was writing at a time of colonial expansion, as European powers explored the world, built empires and developed the slave trade. The central character, Oroonoko, is a black African prince caught up in the slave traffic to America.

The title page is also intriguing in the claim it makes about the sort of text it is: a 'true history'. Some people believe it is pure fiction; others have gone in search of evidence that Aphra Behn spent time in Africa, establishing a factual basis for her tale. As we argued in Chapter 1, our distinction between 'history' and fiction has been in many ways a very twentieth century concern. We should note, however, that she does not call her text a 'novel'.

Nor does Daniel Defoe. His texts are described as 'memorandums' (*Moll Flanders*) and a 'Life', 'Adventures' and 'Account' (*Robinson Crusoe*). Again, these title pages make claims of truth and authenticity. The name of the writer, Defoe, does not appear. The pretence is that the narrators, Moll and Crusoe, are real people telling their own story or autobiography. Although there was a real sailor, Alexander Selkirk, whose story Defoe drew upon for Crusoe, and speculation about a source for Moll, they are both Defoe's fictional constructs. Defoe worked in trade and journalism, areas flourishing in the eighteenth century, and he was a keen observer of society concerned with economics. Like *Oroonoko*, these histories deal with adventures in far-off lands (Moll travels to America), and the possibilities of movement both geographically and socially were becoming interesting concerns in the society of the eighteenth century.

Like the title pages of *Robinson Crusoe* and *Moll Flanders*, that of *Pamela* seems to give us the whole story on the front page – it lets us know what we're getting. The expectation of who the readers are is also explicit here, the 'Youth of Both Sexes'. The apparent purpose of the text is highly moral, teaching young people the principles of virtue and religion. The book also promises to be 'entertaining'. We, the reader, are assumed to be extremely interested in 'genteel' life and the 'exalted condition'. Like Crusoe, the 'truth' of the account is guaranteed by the 'Editor' who contributes a preface to Pamela's letters. Pamela is a fictitious character, a servant girl who heroically resists the dastardly seductions of her Master until he gives in and marries her. You may have noted that this text takes the form of letters, which give it the illusion of authenticity. Pamela manages to write these letters in all sorts of unlikely situations which became a joke in Henry Fielding's novel, *Shamela*. For example, she carries on writing her letters even though the villainous seducer is getting into bed with her. *Pamela* was a runaway bestseller success, which other writers of the time recognised was well worth imitating or parodying, as Henry Fielding did in *Shamela*. Novels in the form of letters became popular in the eighteenth century and are known as **epistolary** novels, told through epistles or letters. Before modern transport and communications, the letter was extremely important in the lives of people who could read and write. The concept of mobility is important in this novel too, but unlike Defoe's geographical adventures, this is more domestic: social and sexual adventuring.

Another very popular writer at the time, Ann Radcliffe, is not frequently read today. She was a writer of Gothic tales, which we shall return to later in Chapter 5. You probably noticed that this title page for *The Mysteries of Udolpho* is volume one of four volumes. Many texts were published in this way in the eighteenth century and this carried on into the nineteenth century. Readers would be eager to get hold of the next volume. In an era when books were generally extremely expensive, this might involve a considerable outlay of cash. Middle-class readers might belong to a circulating library, but if they wanted to ensure they got all four volumes of *The Mysteries of Udolpho* together, they would have to take out four paid subscriptions, one for each book. The writer's name is not only included on this title page, but the book is 'sold' on her reputation, to the fans of her other works, '*The Romance of The Forest, Etc*'. Many of the writers and readers of Gothic fiction were women and it was a very popular form with both sexes, so has often been regarded as popular, rather than serious literary fiction and therefore marginalised by some critics. This book is explicitly labelled a '**Romance**'. This is the label given to texts which deal with events and characters removed from the everyday world, inherited from medieval tales of courtly love. Yet again this text is not called a 'novel'.

It is not until we look at the title page for *Mansfield Park* that we encounter a text that confidently calls itself a 'novel'. It does not reveal its storyline on the title page, nor give us other clues as to its contents. It is promoted as being written by the author of *Sense and Sensibility* and *Pride and Prejudice*, but no name is given. The author was Jane Austen. Clearly her earlier books were well received as this is a selling point here, but the writer is not deemed important. If you buy a copy of a Jane Austen novel today her name will feature very prominently on the cover and title page. Jane Austen's work as a *novel* is distinguished from the *romance* of Ann Radcliffe. In fact in one of her novels, *Emma*, an Austen character is a keen reader of *The Romance of The Forest*, but this is an implied humorous criticism of her lack of learning and judgement. Austen's novel, *Northanger Abbey* sends up and ridicules the Gothic novels so popular at the end of the eighteenth century. Ann Radcliffe, who put her name on the title page, got £500 for *The Mysteries of Udolpho*. Austen got £10 for *Northanger Abbey*. But it is Jane Austen who is the more highly-regarded and widely-read writer today.

ACTIVITY 8

1 Look again at the novels you are studying as set texts for your course and think critically about how they are presented and packaged for the reader. Look at the cover, title pages and back cover.

What do the cover design and the 'blurbs' suggest about the kind of text it is and the kind of reader it expects to attract?

If you are studying older texts, try to find out how the book looked when it was first sold. You could search the Web, or visit The British Library or other museums with first editions. Some of the editions you use will give you a facsimile of the original title page.

What does it tell you and how does it differ from the modern title page?

2 Design a title page for a text you are studying that informs the reader about the text, classifies the text, summarises the text's contents and intentions and implies who it is written for. For eighteenth and nineteenth century texts you should adopt the style of punctuation and spelling as far as possible, that is lots of capital letters and use of *f* in place of *s*. You will need to look at originals to work out how this is done.

If you are studying modern texts, the preliminary pages can seem quite plain and boring.

Look at the contents page from a twenty-first century novel. What is unusual and interesting here? What does it suggest about the text and the reader?

House of Leaves Contents Page

The contents page adopts a very playful attitude towards the text and the reader. We will be looking at this much more fully when we examine post-modern writing in Chapter 7. What we have seen in this analysis of preliminary pages is that eighteenth century texts were also playful in their ideas about texts and readers. The title page of the Jane Austen novel is the most similar to the mass of novels we read now. Many accounts of the novel seem to tell a story of how books like Jane Austen's came to be seen as the mainstream novel form, how we expect a novel to behave. This is the story of **realism** and it is a very important story to examine when we think about the novel.

Telling the story of the novel

ACTIVITY 9

Read the following section which is about *An Introduction to the English Novel* written by the critic Arnold Kettle and includes extracts from his book (printed in italics).

In a small group, go through the extracts from Kettle's book.

Summarise his argument by putting them in short bullet points in your own words.

What interests you in his attitudes towards the novel, towards history and towards male and female readers and writers?

The time has come to pose explicitly our first essential problem: why did the modern novel arise at all?

The answer can be put in a number of ways. The novel, we may say, arose as a realistic reaction to the medieval romance and its courtly descendants of the sixteenth and seventeenth centuries; the great eighteenth century novels are nearly all anti-romances. Or the novel, we may say, arose with the growth for the first time of a large widely distributed reading public; with the increase of literacy the demand for reading material naturally rose and the demand was greatest among well-to-do women who were the insatiable novel-readers of the time. For such a public, spread all over England in country houses, the theatre was not a feasible form of entertainment, but the novel was perfection. Hence the length of the novels (for their readers had only too much time on their hands), hence their tone, hence their number, hence (by the end of the eighteenth century) the circulating libraries. Or the novel, we may say, grew with the middle class, a new art form based not on aristocratic patronage but on commercial publishing, an art-form written by and for the now-powerful bourgeoisie.

These answers are all part of the truth, but they are less than the whole of it. The whole answer cannot be condensed into a sentence and is as hard to grasp as history itself. We shall not understand the rise of the English novel unless we understand the meaning and importance of the English Revolution of the seventeenth century.

Kettle goes on to examine the impact of the changes in society in the seventeenth century. His argument is that the novel developed as an important form at the time when feudalism, the medieval view of society as fixed and hierarchical, with people born into their place and recognising their bonds and duties to those above and below them in rank – monarchy at the top and peasants at the bottom, was replaced by early capitalism. This is where economic relationships are rooted in market forces, such as buying and selling, whereas supply and demand and social relationships are more determined by class and division of labour. Obviously, a change like this does not occur overnight, nor is there a simple switch from one form of social and economic organisation to another. Kettle argues that the rise of the 'bourgeoisie', the middle class, with its commercial concerns and its culture of individualism whereby individuals like Moll Flanders or Crusoe can pursue their own interests, is very important for the novel. This new social class needed to separate itself from the Romance of feudalism:

'And it explains why in eighteenth century England there should have been a particular impulse towards prose-writing. For Literature to the bourgeois writers of this period was, above all, a means of taking stock of the new society. A medium which could express a realistic and objective curiosity about man and his world, this was what they were after.... They were themselves revolutionaries only in the sense that they participated in the consequences of a revolution; they were more free and therefore more realistic than their predecessors to just the extent and in just those ways that the English bourgeois revolution involved in fact an increase in human freedom.'

Arnold Kettle was a Marxist critic (see Chapter 5) who was very interested in relating novels to historical social class relationships. He uses the term 'realistic' here in a way that suggests the novel was much truer to experience. He seems to assume that the novelist is male and the reader a rich female with too much leisure time. His view was that the novel was a form which could criticise society and contribute towards 'human freedom.' What do you think of this idea?

There have been a number of other writers who have told the story of the novel. Another very influential book was Ian Watt's *The Rise of the Novel*. Like Kettle, Watt was a Marxist who traced the development of the form to the increasingly secular (non-religious) and individualistic culture of the eighteenth century. The writers he focuses on are male. Both Kettle and Watt have been very influential in the way we regard the novel, but the problem with a title like *The Rise of . . .* is that it can, perhaps, tell an untroubled story. If telling a story is fundamental to our way of understanding and communicating, then when we tell the story of the novel we give it a beginning, a middle and an end. Some writers have talked about the death of the novel in the twentieth century, as if the story is finished with now. (We will consider this again in Chapter 7). The story of the novel we tell might include some characters and perspectives but not others. It will have a point of view. It will unfold a sequence.

Clearly there is a danger in describing a literary form as a continuous tradition. Other writers, for example, have argued that Watt and Kettle propose a male-centred tradition. Some feminist scholarship has described an alternative to this patrilineage (tradition of male writers following each other) and proposed a matrilineage of women writers. Others have disputed the English-centeredness of such accounts of the novel as excluding the work of writers from outside Western Europe, or writers from the colonies such as India, which were yoked into an English-centred literary culture through the education and missionary work that issued from the Empire, disseminating, for example, the Bible and Shakespeare. A book like Margaret Anne Doody's *The True Story of the Novel*, through its provocative title alone reveals the contest and jostling that goes on between theories of the novel. She argues that the novel is not new at all and takes a broader view of prose narrative to pose a history of the form going back 2000 years. It could be argued that the accounts of the development of the novel, such as Watt's and Kettle's, that were established just as the study of literature itself was becoming very well established in the 1950s, were based on an assumption that a certain type of novel was more worth studying. This point takes us back to the concept of realism which we will examine in the next chapter.

The idea of tradition

ACTIVITY 10

Read the following extracts from texts written about the novel and discuss them in small groups, answering the questions that follow.

The first extract is from a book first published in 1948 by the Cambridge critic F. R. Leavis in which he defines *The Great Tradition*. The opening line of the book states, 'The great English novelists are Jane Austen, George Eliot, Henry James and Joseph Conrad ...'. The following extracts are from the first chapter:

It is necessary to insist, then, that there are important distinctions to be made, and that far from all of the names in the literary histories really belong to the realm of significant creative achievement. And as a recall to a due sense of differences it is well to start by distinguishing the few really great – the major novelists who count in the same way as the major poets, in the sense that they not only change the possibilities of the art for practitioners and readers, but that they are significant in terms of the human awareness they promote; awareness of the possibilities of life...

Jane Austen is one of the truly great writers ... (her) plots, and her novels in general, were put together very 'deliberately and calculatedly' (if not 'like a building'). But her interest in 'composition' is not something to be put over against her interest in life; nor does she offer an 'aesthetic' value that is separable

from moral significance. The principle of organisation, and the principle of development, in her work is an intense moral interest of her own in life that is in the first place a preoccupation with certain problems that life compels on her as personal ones. She is intelligent and serious enough to be able to impersonalise her moral tensions as she strives, in her art, to become more fully conscious of them, and to learn what, in the interests of life, she ought to do with them. Without her intense moral preoccupation she wouldn't have been a great novelist.

According to Leavis, what makes a writer qualify as 'great'?

The next extract is taken from *An Introduction to Women's Writing* published in 1998 and Lyn Pykett writes here about the nineteenth century novel in a very different way to Leavis. What interests this writer in telling the story of the novel?

The novel was indisputably the literary form most widely and successfully practised by women in the Victorian period. If one includes those writers who wrote for children, about 80% of all professional women writers in the nineteenth century wrote fiction. John Sutherland's Companion to Victorian Fiction ... contains entries for 878 novelists, of whom 312 are women. The average lifetime production of these women 'breaks down' (as no doubt many of them did under the strain of constant literary production) to 21 titles as compared with 17.6 titles for male novelists. In virtually every decade in the period 1830–80, and certainly from the 1840s onwards, both male and female commentators on the literary scene regularly pronounced that (for good or ill) this was 'the age of female novelists' (Oliphant, 1855) . . . Several of them, and not always those that appear on today's school and university syllabuses, enjoyed notable critical success. Several succeeded in generating considerable sums of money for their publishers, if not always for themselves, by producing bestsellers. However, it is also the case that, as Nigel Cross has noted, 'no sooner had fiction writing become the most profitable form of literary activity, in the 1840s, than men began to outnumber women in the fiction publisher's lists' (Cross, 1985).

Throughout its history there has been a close connection between the novel and women, and,

more complexly, between fiction and a culturally constructed idea of the feminine. From its emergence in the eighteenth century and throughout the period 1830–80, the form and subject matter of fiction, the means by which it was produced and distributed, and the social and critical debates it generated were complexly but inextricably interconnected with women's establishment of themselves as professional writers, with the growth of a female reading public, and with ideas (or a contestation of ideas) about femininity. As several recent literary historians have argued, the development of the novel in the eighteenth century not only permitted the entry of women into the writing profession, but it was also associated with a feminisation of literature and culture; a process by which literature became increasingly defined 'as a special category supposedly outside the political arena, with an influence on the world as indirect as women's was supposed to be' (Spencer, 1986).

COMMENTARY Leavis writes in a very authoritative way and insists on the importance of making judgements about the merits and importance of novelists. The merits he looks for are aesthetic – that the novel is beautifully written, and moral – that it has a serious purpose in developing 'human awareness'. He dismisses writers of comic novels like Henry Fielding as lacking 'classical distinction' and Laurence Sterne's work as 'irresponsible (and nasty) trifling'. Terms like *originality, perfection, genius* are important in this chapter as Leavis is also concerned with establishing a line that links the writers he regards as great, following the idea that all writers necessarily read and transform the work of earlier writers. The poet, T.S. Eliot, had argued that bad writers 'borrow' but good writers 'steal', meaning that good writers make the tradition their own; they pick it up and take it somewhere else.

Lyn Pykett has a very different approach. Instead of writing about intrinsic qualities of literary form or the merits and moral positions of writers, she is interested in providing statistics that describe the production of texts. She quotes information from a variety of sources to support her points. The historical connections she presents are not those of one individual genius reading the work of another, but are concerned with the changing processes of culture and in particular the way women's relationship to the novel shapes ideas about texts and about society. Pykett is examining the novel from a feminist and cultural materialist position (see Chapter 5), arguing that the novel is not only *about* society, as Leavis suggests, but *part* of the processes of change in a society. In this case, she suggests that changing attitudes towards women are tied up in shifting attitudes towards literary texts. The approach Leavis takes is interested only in the texts themselves and he regards them as outside of society, commenting on it. Their important relationship, for Leavis, is with the texts of other great writers.

Do you find one of these approaches more interesting, challenging or useful than the other?

Telling the story of a novel

ACTIVITY 11

Research the reviews that your set texts received when they were first published. Identify what the critics praised and criticised at the time and discuss together whether the critical reception of the text has changed over time. In pairs or small groups prepare a presentation or wall display that tells the story of your set text's critical past. Many canonical texts, such as those by Austen, Dickens, Eliot or Hardy will have extensive material on internet sites as well as in books such as *The Critical Heritage* series which provide the views of critics from when the texts were written, up until the present day. It is particularly interesting to see the contemporary debates around novels such as those by the Brontë sisters or Mary Shelley where the writers 'hid' their true identities.

In this chapter you have started to examine the novel in terms of genre and context. You have considered the development of the form in the eighteenth and nineteenth century and the differing accounts that may be offered of this development. Historical factors are important to consider, not only because they shape forms of prose narrative, but also because histories are themselves formed in narrative.

3 Exploring Narrative Fiction

This chapter invites you to consider the formal aspects of prose texts that you will be likely to consider in your studies. Some you will be familiar with, such as characterisation and use of setting. Other approaches here have been influenced by developments in narratology – the systematic study of narrative. We will also draw on reader-response theories which have examined concepts such as the implied reader. In this chapter, therefore, we will look both *in* on the text's construction and *out* from the text to the reader. To start with, we will consider the idea that what we look at when we examine novels may, in fact, be subject to change.

The examiner's agenda

ACTIVITY 12

Look at the following questions taken from examination papers.

■ Pick out the key words in each question and in your own words explain what the question wants the candidate to do.
■ What assumptions underlie each question about the ways students will have been studying the novel?
■ Which questions seem most familiar to you?
■ Do some seem very different from the sorts of questions you might expect?

Some are from the 1960s, others from the early 1990s, others are for 2001. Can you tell?

1 'That cumbersome piece of machinery, the plot.' How far does interest in the plot contribute to the artistic success or failure of Jane Austen?

2 Discuss the work of any novelist or essayist who seems to you to be a great writer either because of the importance of his ideas or because of the distinction of his prose style.

3 Illustrate from any eighteenth-century author how the events and conditions of his own life are reflected in his writings.

4 Have you any sympathy for Alec d'Urberville in Thomas Hardy's *Tess of the d'Urbervilles*?

5 Look at Chapter 11 of *The Secret Agent*. What are your feelings about Winnie Verloc in this chapter? How does Conrad make you see her as you do?

6 Hardy gave his novel *Tess of the d'Urbervilles* the sub-title *A Pure Woman*. Does his portrayal of Tess convince you of her essential purity?

7 Remind yourself of Sarah's prayer on page 93 of Graham Greene's *The End of the Affair*. Then answer all three parts of the question.
   i) How does Greene present the character of Sarah here?
   ii) How does this prayer affect our response to Sarah elsewhere in the novel?

iii) Readers find Sarah either a saint or a whore. What is your opinion of her?

8 With close reference to two or three episodes, discuss the ways in which Shelley makes the novel *Frankenstein*, a criticism of the society of the time.

In your answer you should consider the following aspects:

- the portrayal of the family
- the use made in the narrative of particular examples of injustice, inhumanity and abuse of power
- the importance of money and position

COMMENTARY   Questions 1, 2 and 3 came from papers sat by A level students wanting to enter Cambridge University in the early years of the 1960s. You may have noticed how the wording of the questions ('success' or 'failure', 'great' or 'distinction') encourages the judgements of texts as part of the canon and assumes the confidence of students in describing such 'qualities' in literature. You may detect the influence of Cambridge don, F.R. Leavis's approach which we examined in the last chapter in this book. Question 3, however, from the same source, gives importance to the biography of the writer. Following debates about the 'death' of the author (along the lines of 'the meaning is present only in the text') and the canon (along the lines of 'there is no such thing as an objective assessment') these questions gave way to other types of question. Questions 2 and 3 assume that the writer is male.

Those from the early 1990s (4,5,and 6) focus much more on the reader's response. They encourage the reader to identify with the characters as if they were real people.

You may well have identified questions 7 and 8 as being the most similar to the type of questions you will answer in your examinations. These questions are helpful in focusing your attention on the assessment objectives. In Chapter 8 of this book you will look again at what examination questions are asking you to do. Use the assessment objectives which are given in that chapter to analyse which AOs are being targeted in these two questions.

We can see from this that, like everything else, attitudes towards the analysis of prose constantly change. If you were writing about a novel a hundred years ago, you might, perhaps, have concentrated on the biographical details of the author – the kind of approach that is still evident in question 3 above. Fifty years ago you might have focused on the structure and language of the text and considered its merits as in questions 1 and 2. Ten years ago your focus might have been on your interaction with the text. Today you might write about the text's relationship to other texts, or examine it in its historical context or discuss the response of different readers to it. There is no universally fixed set of guidelines for examining prose texts. Any book that tells you how to study a novel will need to be revised years later as approaches to texts and to literary study develop. What you must do is examine the agenda of the questions set by your examination specification. We will return to this in Chapter 8.

Analysing narrative structure

Many of the studies of fiction in recent decades have been concerned with examining the elements of narrative and in particular, distinguishing between the story of a text and the ways the events are told, often called the **discourse**. Of course these are not separate ingredients in a text, but work together in very interesting ways. You might find the following checklist of questions helpful when analysing the narrative structure of your set books.

Questions

Events

What are the main events – the key things that happen in the text?

Storyline

How are these events told? Perhaps in chronological order as they might have happened in time?

Does the text move backwards and forwards over the time span of the events?

Is a key event held back or kept secret until the end – such as in detective novels? Are there significant gaps in the telling, long periods of time that are passed over?

Discourse

Who tells the story? Is it a first, second (rarely) or third person narration? Is there an all-knowing (omniscient) narrator or one who sees the events from a particular point of view?

What is the narrator's relationship to the story – remote or involved – in what way?

How does the text invite the reader to regard the narrator, for example as trustworthy or unreliable or unsympathetic?

What seems to be the medium of the narration – e.g. does it sound like spoken or written language?

Events and storyline

In any complex text such as those you are likely to be studying, there will be a great deal more going on than the skeleton of the events that you identify as the key things that happen. In *Wuthering Heights* by Emily Brontë, for example, both the storyline, which moves back and forth in time, dwelling on some events and slipping over (or eliding) others, and the use of different narrators who see the events only from their own perspective, serve to make the novel a very interesting and challenging text for readers to find their way through.

ACTIVITY 13

If you are familiar with *Wuthering Heights*, or alternatively using a set text you know well, try drawing two charts. One should be a simple chronological timeline showing the main events in the order in which they occurred in time. The other chart should represent the narrative – starting at the beginning of the text and moving through. This should show the order in which events are told or revealed and by whom. This is best done in small groups.

When you have completed the charts, see what you notice about:

- the gaps in the text – what isn't revealed?
- which events get extensive treatment?
- which events are revisited?

Ask yourselves why and see what points you can make about the patterns, connections or lack of connections as you compare the charts.

As an example, the diagrams on the following pages show some students using diagrams to work on a late twentieth century novel, *Behind the Scenes at the Museum*, by Kate Atkinson. The narrative is complicated, as the narrator ranges backwards and forwards over the generations of a family spanning 100 years. In the first diagram (which works from bottom to top) the students drew a chronological timeline of events in the novel over that period and the winding pattern of arrows on the right records the events as they were recounted in the text. This chart examines how the novel intersects public events with family ones, locating the personal story in historical experience and making connections that cut across time. The second diagram is a tree of relationships. Both charts suggested to the students that neither history nor family could be adequately described by the neat organising principles of simple timelines or family trees and that the very complexity of patterns was a central part of the meaning of the novel. It also enabled them to make many connections and recognise the highly wrought structuring of the text.

Storyline and discourse

It is interesting to try writing yourself to see what happens when you disrupt the chronological order of a story and how this affects the telling of the story.

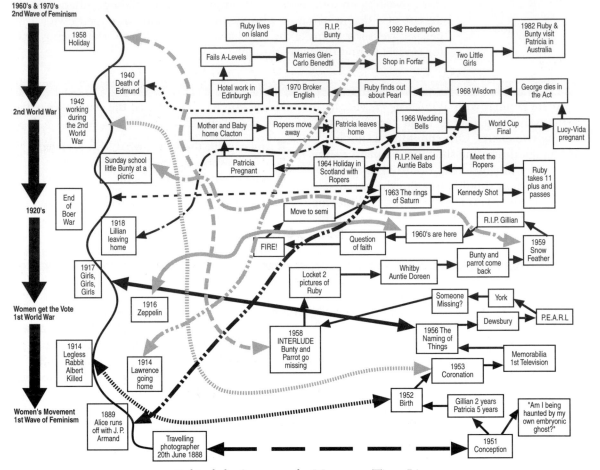

Behind the Scenes at the Museum – Time Line

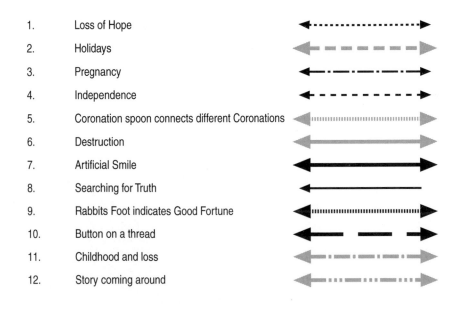

1.	Loss of Hope	
2.	Holidays	
3.	Pregnancy	
4.	Independence	
5.	Coronation spoon connects different Coronations	
6.	Destruction	
7.	Artificial Smile	
8.	Searching for Truth	
9.	Rabbits Foot indicates Good Fortune	
10.	Button on a thread	
11.	Childhood and loss	
12.	Story coming around	

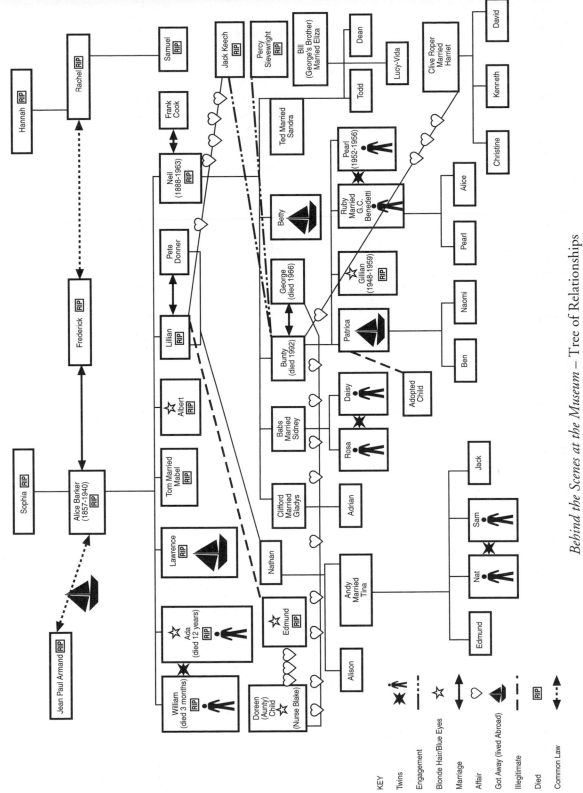

Behind the Scenes at the Museum – Tree of Relationships

ACTIVITY 14

Ask your partner, or choose for yourself, a number from 1 to 7. Write it down before reading on.

The following is a series of events given in the order in which they happened. This is allegedly 'true' (I did get this listening to a Radio 4 programme!!).

1 Person A falls ill with heart disease and needs a transplant.
2 Person B is murdered.
3 Person A is given B's heart in the transplant operation.
4 As person A comes around from the operation, s/he experiences 'memories' of the murder.
5 Person A gives information to the police based on these fragments of memories.
6 The murderer of B is caught by the police following the information.
7 Radio 4 makes a programme about the story.

Before writing

Think about your characters, A and B. Give them a name.

Your task is to write the story starting **from the number you chose**.

You will have to make decisions about the best way to tell the story. For example:

Will you use first person narration (I) or third person (he/she/they)?

Will you use dialogue or reported speech, or get 'inside' a character's mind through an interior monologue or stream of consciousness (thought processes as they happen)?

What style will be most appropriate to your starting point?

After writing

Compare your pieces of writing.

What restrictions and possibilities did your starting point entail?

What do you notice about the difference in narration, form, voice, point of view or conventions of genre that you used?

Students who tried this found that they assumed very different discourses depending on their starting point. Here are some brief extracts from their work, which they had to produce very quickly. Read them and discuss what kind of narrator and discourse they have adopted. Which do you think has the most potential as a starting point for a short story or for a novel?

Student A

I sit slumped on the broken green office chair, salvaged a few weeks ago. I hate this chair, its sickening lustre reminding me of my mother's house. I stare at the cigarette in my trembling hand and move to the window to dispose of it through the shattered pane. Kids scream and dance around each other under the grey skies, revelling in their innocence, unaware of the presence outside my door. My letterbox is pushed open by a fat finger and then snapped shut. I hear deep voices and scan my surroundings for an escape. Eight stories up there is no escape. Deep breath. Open eyes. Open door. Can I help you, Officer?

Student B

'I hope to God this works.'

'Alright, I've done it. Quick.... Give it everything you've got, Tom, or we'll lose him.'

Surgeon Thomas Wheeler grabbed the heart resuscitation kit with some reluctance, and immediately applied it to the chest of the patient.

'CLEAR!'

Pressing down with all his might, Wheeler was always amazed at his own heart rate more so than the patient's ... it was thumping heavily in his chest with the desperation of getting it right. The life of this man was in his hands now – every second was crucial.

'CLEAR!'

Student C

Quite a remarkable story this morning. A man has been arrested in connection with the murder of Brian Harvey outside Huddersfield Community Church. He was shot in the head by a masked gunman who made his exit in a blue jeep. Police gained information on the murder from Annika Abdely whose diseased heart was replaced by Mr Harvey's three weeks ago. Strange though it may seem, Miss Abdely could recall enough evidence after recuperation to lead to the arrest of the gunman. This is a twenty-first century miracle which has left coronary experts around the country dumbfounded.

Student A, starting from number 6, used the historic present tense to create a sense of immediacy and offered the interior monologue of the murderer. Student B's piece used omniscient narration and moved between different characters, using a lot of dialogue in his piece, starting from number 3. Student C wrote the radio presenter's script for number 7 and included a number of interviews in the report.

Characters and discourse

In the writing exercise, the point at which the students entered the storyline imposed limits on the way they could tell the story and the characters they could use. Many of them found themselves imitating certain familiar styles or discourses, influenced, for example, by the dialogue of TV police or hospital programmes like *The Bill* or *Casualty*, or by the register of well-known radio presenters. In the following activity you will look more carefully at the way the use of characters and different discourses can affect the reader.

ACTIVITY 15

In pairs, look carefully at the following extracts. They are all dealing with the experiences of slavery on the American plantations in the late 1700s or early 1800s. Copy the following chart onto a piece of paper. Discuss the narration of each passage and note down your observations on the narration using the headings. Include any other ideas or thoughts you have as you work together on the passages.

Extract Number:	Medium: written/ spoken? public/ private? What effect?	What type of text do you think it is? What does it remind you of?	Narrator: 1st, 2nd, 3rd person? What effect?	Tense: past or present? What effect?	Style of telling and characteristics of narrator?	Your response? Effect on reader?
1						
2						
3						
4						
5						

1 I leave the plantation for one night and a day, one night and a day, that's all, and I return to virtual chaos. Overseer, you were supposed to supervise. Deputy you are paid to work for me and do as I say on my plantation. . . . Your son, God rest his agitated soul, has brought calamity on my head. He is dead through his own design. Thank God my wife and daughter were not present to witness the debacle. His action was rebellion of the most heinous kind. Had he survived, his life on the plantation would have been finished. You yourself have said that a slave who has tasted liberty can never be a proper slave again.

2 May 27
The runaway is back. It transpires he was hiding in an abandoned cottage a few miles North of here waiting for a group of other runaways heading north, but they did not materialise. He just walked back through the main gates, looking haggard and hungry. A shame he did not allow someone to grab him a few miles out and get that reward. He got 200 lashes. I administered half, my second the rest. His back was raw. He had to be revived twice from a dead faint. All were present and seemed suitably appalled and discouraged from imitating him.

3 *My father is the oldest man in the world.*
I am his only son, not his thirteenth girl.

My mother is an angel without wings,
Fallen from grace, the sun has smoked her skin.

But she is lovely within; a pure light
Radiates from her; though black, her soul is white.

She is young enough to be his granddaughter
In which case I could call him Great grandfather.

He washed me with his great grandchildren,
Every day, at dusk, except on Sundays when

He supervised our wash in the morning for church.
He led us there and back with a piece of birch

Which he slapped on his left trouser leg
With each step of his left foot; us on edge

All the way there and back, afraid to laugh
Out loud and talking in whispers; I was his calf.

That birch I had to pick was never used
On me, never; it hung over me like a noose

I had no intention of putting round my neck
By behavior I knew that birch would check.

4 What brings me here? My need to be ridiculed. My search for vindication. My confusion. I know the questions because I am about to ask them. The answers are mine too but I need to hear the words from a mouth I can watch.

You own the Whitechapel plantation. Your father helped to build this club. You walk through the front door as if you are home. The floorboards under your feet welcome you with their familiar creak. Dust between those boards is yours as well as your father's. You are here because there is nowhere else. Home, the boards chatter, welcome home, as you head for the main lounge relieved of your coat, stick and hat by a slave you did not see you are so wrapped up in yourself.

5 The Virginian, Editorial, February 4, 1810

If slaves are stock should we be concerned about the sale of a woman and her children that might very well result in their separation? This good question raises a philosophical enquiry into the degree of humanity we should accord slaves. Are we to attribute to slaves all the qualities we credit to ourselves as human beings? I think not.

The premise of buying and selling of Africans is built upon precepts concerning their difference from our good selves. They are, quite literally, not like us. They do not feel what we feel. They do not value what we value. They will exhibit habits of attachment not unlike those observed among other kinds of stock on the plantation: a cow's to its newborn calf; a mare's to its foal.

It is wise not to confuse such displays of attachment and habit of love. At the auction block, get the best price for your investment even if it means breaking up the capital into smaller holdings and selling each holding separately.

COMMENTARY In fact, all these extracts came from one novel, *The Longest Memory*. The writer, the black British poet Fred D'Aguiar, constructs his narrative around one main event, the whipping to death of a slave called Chapel. This event is approached and continually re-approached from different chronological and narrative directions. Each chapter in the book changes the perspective of the reader, positioning the reader differently according to the different speaker's involvement in the story. The hierarchy of the society is represented in this polyphonic (many voiced) text, from the male white plantation owner to the male white employee, the white woman, the black male slave down to the black female slave. In the extracts you examined above, 1 and 4 are narrated by Mr Whitechapel, the plantation owner. 1 is in his public mode, addressing his slave and overseer; 4 is his private interior voice, characterised by such a divided self that he splits into two, the YOU and the I. This device dramatises the conflict he feels because he does not identify with the other, more brutal slave owners. The newspaper editor of *The Virginian* in 5 adopts the seemingly dispassionate language of authority, but of course the chilling logic of such convincing rhetoric is revealed as appallingly cruel. In the novel, the newspaper editorials comment plausibly on the institution and practices of slavery and its critics, but are also entwined with the events of the death of Chapel on the plantation, showing how individual private histories intersect with public debate. The overseer who narrates through a diary in extract 2 is a callous figure, but also a marginalised one, without much authority. A diary is appropriate for him: he lacks a public voice, but he is also a keeper of vital secrets. The poetry is part of the text 'spoken' by Chapel, the slave who is born of a black woman raped by the overseer and who dies from the beating. Chapel is earlier punished for learning to read. His white lover, Lydia, teaches him the literary classics such as Shakespeare and Milton. Chapel is expressed here in the form of 'high' English poetry – the rhymed iambic couplet. His language is haunted by biblical and literary ideas which he was denied because of his position as slave and had to acquire subversively. Although he takes on this language, he has no other voice in the text.

This technique, of multiple narration – many tellers of the same story, has interested quite a few novelists. What D'Aguiar also does here, which is perhaps more unusual, is to disrupt the discourse so that the text varies in form from diaries to newspaper editorials, dramatic monologues to interior monologues, narrated debates to poetry. We move between the public rhetoric of powerful speakers and writers, like the plantation owners and the newspaper editor, and the private confessionals of the slaves and the women, black and white, who are powerless and dispossessed. Rather than identify with characters and empathise with the situation, the reader is constantly being displaced and invited to debate the issues and examine how language and discourses construct the institution, history and experiences of slavery.

The work of the reader in examining texts

Texts like the ones we have looked at in this chapter, *Wuthering Heights, Behind the Scenes at the Museum* and *The Longest Memory* all seem to demand a lot of work from the reader. There has been a great deal of interest in recent decades in the ways that readers make meaning from texts. Some reader-response critics would argue that there are as many versions of one text as there are readers of it, because every reader makes their own unique interpretation of it. Readers are not blank slates onto which a text is inscribed. Every reader brings to every text their own experiences and reading histories. Some of these may well be shared. If you have been through a similar education system, or occupy a similar cultural position (consider factors like age, gender, race, class) you are likely to be part of an 'interpretive community' who look at texts in particular ways. In fact if A level students were not like this, the course might be very different or take much longer! One of the words used in the assessment objectives is 'respond': at AS level you are expected to be active and self-conscious in your reading and at A2 be able to evaluate your own readings against others. One of the ways of tuning in to your responses is to slow down and identify your thoughts as you read and consider how they arose.

ACTIVITY 16

Take a short section of a text you are studying. Photocopy it and stick it onto a large sheet of paper. Working very slowly through the text, record your thoughts around it, attaching comments to parts of the text. Think not only about the detail in the text but also about the ideas you bring to it. You can then try comparing your 'text' with someone else's 'text'. If you do this in a group, you can add comments to each other's comments in different colours. Ask yourselves whether you are a reading community at peace or in conflict!

On page 34 is an example of one student working closely with an extract from *Wuthering Heights*. This example is interesting because it imitates the way the character, Cathy, wrote around the margins of books. It is around the edges that she tries to make meaning, so that's what this student was trying to do!

In recent years reading groups have become popular in America and the UK, keenly supported as you might expect, by the book industry. Look on pages 35 and 36 where there are examples of leaflets put out by publishing houses on novels they think would be suitable for discussion in reading groups.

What kind of reader have they got in mind here?
How do they expect the reader to approach texts?

ACTIVITY 17

Take one of your set texts that you know well. As a group, produce a reading group leaflet for that text. You may wish to follow the format shown on pages 35 and 36 quite closely, including a summary of the text, key questions to discuss and further reading. You may want to produce something more imaginative!

Implied readers

All texts, whatever they might be, whether novels, publishers' leaflets, computer manuals, holiday brochures or football programmes have real readers, the people who at a particular moment are reading that text. They also have implied readers, the position they assume the reader to occupy. For example, the implied reader of Watford FC's programme for the match against Gillingham, is a follower of the game, highly informed about the excellent quality of the home team. The real reader may, in fact, have no interest in football at all but is interested in layout and design for a programme for something else. With fiction, the text can set up a model of the kind of reader it expects and the reader can accommodate him or

It must say something about Emily Brontë's opinion on organised religion, that not only is Lockwood's nightmare about religion but also Catherine seems to have no respect for the religious book she writes her diary on.

Even Lockwood, a respectable city gentleman finds the religious books repressive.

He must have been shocked and surprised at the extent of which the children were subjected to them, otherwise they would never have played such a large part of his dreams, in such a negative way.

Lockwood, now awake and able to look back calls his dreams 'curious'. This is a vastly under-exaggerated comment, but Lockwood would almost certainly believe it to be a human fault to be influenced in sleep by a young girl's diary. He has a very high opinion of himself and rather fancies himself in the role of a romantic hero.

Disillusioned is the word that springs to mind regarding Lockwood.

'A diary in the margins'. Catherine is writing her diary in the margins of any book she can find on the shelves in her room. This reminds me of a story I once heard about a prisoner who was forced to write his autobiography around articles in a newspaper, for want of better paper. Some may argue, Catherine is no more fortunate than this prisoner.

WUTHERING HEIGHTS

forted, we each sought a separate nook to await his advent.

'I reached this book, and a pot of ink from the shelf, and pushed the house-door ajar to give me light, and I have got the time on with writing for twenty minutes; but my companion is impatient and proposes that we should appropriate the dairy woman's cloak, and have a scamper on the moors, under its shelter. A pleasant suggestion – and then, if the surly old man come in, he may believe his prophecy verified – we cannot be damper, or colder, in the rain than we are here.'

I suppose Catherine fulfilled her project, for the next sentence took up another subject: she waxed lachrymose.

'How little did I dream that Hindley would ever make me cry so!' she wrote. 'My head aches, till I cannot keep it on the pillow; and still I can't give over. Poor Heathcliff! Hindley calls him a vagabond, and won't let him sit with us, nor eat with us any more; and, he says, he and I must not play together, and threatens to turn him out of the house if we break his orders.

'He has been blaming our father (how dared he?) for treating H. too liberally; and swears he will reduce him to his right place –'

•

I began to nod drowsily over the dim page; my eye wandered from manuscript to print. I saw a red ornamental title – 'Seventy Times Seven, and the First of the Seventy-First. A Pious Discourse delivered by the Reverend Jabes Branderham, in the Chapel of Gimmerden Sough.' And while I was, half consciously, worrying my brain to guess what Jabes Branderham would make of his subject, I sank back in bed, and fell asleep.

Alas, for the effects of bad tea and bad temper! what else could it be that made me pass such a terrible night? I don't remember another that I can at all compare with it since I was capable of suffering.

I began to dream, almost before I ceased to be sensible of my locality. I thought it was morning; and I had to set out on

64

WUTHERING HEIGHTS

my way home, with Joseph for a guide. The snow lay yards deep in our road; and, as we floundered on, my companion wearied me with constant reproaches that I had not brought a pilgrim's staff: telling me that I could never get into the house without one, and boastfully flourishing a heavy-handed cudgel, which I understood to be so denominated.

For a moment I considered it absurd that I should need such a weapon to gain admittance into my own residence. Then, a new idea flashed across me. I was not going there; we were journeying to hear the famous Jabes Branderham preach from the text – 'Seventy Times Seven'; and either Joseph, the preacher, or I had committed the 'First of the Seventy-First,' and were to be publicly exposed and excommunicated.

We came to the chapel – I have passed it really in my walks, twice or thrice: it lies in a hollow, between two hills – an elevated hollow – near a swamp, whose peaty moisture is said to answer all the purposes of embalming on the few corpses deposited there. The roof has been kept whole hitherto; but, as the clergyman's stipend is only twenty pounds per annum, and a house with two rooms, threatening speedily to determine into one, no clergyman will undertake the duties of pastor, especially as it is currently reported that his flock would rather let him starve than increase the living by one penny from their own pockets. However, in my dream, Jabes had a full and attentive congregation: and he preached – good God – what a sermon! divided into *four hundred and ninety* parts, each fully equal to an ordinary address from the pulpit and each discussing a separate sin! Where he searched for them, I cannot tell: he had his private manner of interpreting the phrase, and it seemed necessary the brother should sin different sins on every occasion.

They were of the most curious character – odd transgressions that I never imagined previously.

Oh, how weary I grew. How I writhed, and yawned, and nodded, and revived! How I pinched and pricked myself, and rubbed my eyes, and stood up, and sat down again, and nudged Joseph to inform me if he would *ever* have done! I was condemned to hear all out – finally, he reached the 'First

65

Catherine quite obviously despises her brother Hindley for his vicious treatment of Heathcliff. Heathcliff is treated very badly and alienated from the rest of the family. Catherine feels Hindley is betraying their father in the despicable way Heathcliff is being bullied.

Catherine is driven to tears by the unfair treatment of Heathcliff. This force of feeling although perhaps not too unusual, does provoke some questioning. Others argue 'Why bring sex into everything' and claim the two were drawn into companionship by unbearable outside influences.

Ellen Moers in her book 'Ideas from Literary Women' insists that even at their age Catherine and Heathcliff were experiencing love of an unfraternal kind and certainly sexual in its nature.

Lockwood soon starts to fall asleep on the diary. As he does so, he glimpses the religious title of the book Catherine has written around. This image reinforces the idea of books in the novel. He reads the real print but the manuscript blurs. The confusion of these books induces a horrific nightmare, which, in true Lockwood fashion he puts down to 'bad tea and temper'.

Toni Morrison

Toni Morrison was born Chloe Anthony Wofford, in Ohio in 1931. She studied English and Classics at Howard University, before receiving a master's degree from Cornell University in 1955. After teaching at, among others, Texas Southern University, she became a senior editor at Random House and began writing journalism. She is currently Robert F. Goheen Professor, Council of Humanities, Princeton University.

Toni Morrison is one of the most acclaimed living American writers. The bestselling *Song of Solomon* won the National Book Critic's Circle Award in 1978, and *Beloved* won the Pulitzer Prize in 1988. Her appointment by President Carter to the National Council on the Arts in 1980 was closely followed by her election to the American Academy and Institute of Arts and Letters. In 1993, she won the Nobel Prize for Literature.

To re-order ISBN: 009975021X
Written by Nick Riddle

Vintage is an imprint of Random House,
20 Vauxhall Bridge Road,
London SW1V 2SA
Tel: 0171 840 8400

Beloved
by Toni Morrison

ISBN: 0099760118

About this guide

The questions, discussion topics, and author biography that follow are intended to enhance your group's reading of Toni Morrison's *Beloved*. We hope that they will assist your understanding of this classic of twentieth-century American literature. The narrative mixes past and present, making a straightforward plot summary impossible. The novel opens in Cincinnati, 1873. Sethe and her surviving daughter, Denver, are left to contend with the ghost of Sethe's murdered baby after her two sons flee the house. The arrival of Paul D evokes memories of Sweet Home, the estate in Kentucky where they both worked as slaves. Sethe escaped while she was pregnant with Denver, her three other children having gone on ahead of her to 124 Bluestone Road, the house of Baby Suggs, Sethe's mother-in-law. She gave birth to Denver on the way. Twenty-eight days after her arrival at 124, men from Sweet Home came to take her back. Rather than let her children fall into the hands of the slaveowners, she killed her eldest daughter. As a consequence she went to prison with Denver. Sethe, Denver and Paul D (who is now living with Sethe) find a young black woman outside 124. She calls herself Beloved –the name Sethe had carved on her baby's tombstone–and is taken in by them. Denver is devoted to her, but Paul D is distrustful. He leaves after Stamp Paid tells him of Sethe's crime. The three women withdraw into a world of their own; Sethe is convinced that Beloved is her daughter and begins to waste away from trying to assuage her guilt, while Beloved grows fatter. Denver resolves to break the deadlock; through her the community hears of Sethe's condition and is determined to banish Beloved.

For discussion

1) *Beloved* has many elements often found in ghost stories – the haunted house, the vengeful spirit, the hostile community. What distinguishes *Beloved* from the generic ghost story?

2) Sethe feels that her brain is 'loaded with the past and hungry for more.' (p. 70). What are the dangers to her of this, and what, if any, are the consolations? Does the future exist for her at all?

3) What does *Beloved* have to say about community – its value, its demands, and the relationship of individuals to it?

4) In what ways does Paul D stand out from the other male characters? Does *Beloved* offer a consistent view of the relations between men and women in this period of black American history?

5) Sethe's protective feelings towards Denver are powerful (p.45, p.99), and her nurturing instincts are strong. The novel's central event, however, is Sethe's murder of her own child ('She had to be safe and I put her where she would be,' p.200). How does this revelation affect your view of Sethe?

6) In the early pages of the novel, the spirit world and the material world seem almost indistinguishable. What sort of boundaries exist between the two? How does the belief in a spirit world affect the lives of the characters?

7) How much of a 'person' is Beloved? Given her mysterious arrival and unexplained departure, does she have any reality other than as an embodiment of other people's emotions, e.g. Sethe's guilt?

8) In the course of the novel, Denver begins to discover herself as an individual (p.252). What role does Beloved play in this process?

9) Beloved's emergence from the river (p. 50) is just one of many instances of water imagery. What does water signify in the image-system of the novel, as compared to, say, blood or milk?

10) The narrative of *Beloved* is fragmented, with point-of-view switching between characters and moments in time; yet a sense of order is very much in evidence–see, for instance, the opening sentence of Parts One, Two and Three. What other devices does Toni Morrison use to shape her material?

11) '...definitions belonged to the definers - not the defined.' (p.190) In what ways do the whites use language as a tool of oppression? How do Baby Suggs, Stamp Paid and the others attempt to define themselves?

12) "You got two feet, Sethe, not four." (p.165) Paul D's words initiate a decisive break with Sethe, but their meaning resonates for both of them. Bearing in mind their histories, what special significance does the idea of the 'animal' have for each of them?

13) Baby Suggs' vision of harmony and love is soured by the party she throws and seems to be extinguished at her funeral. (p.171) What does her idealism founder on?

14) Halle is Sethe's husband, but he is notably absent–indeed, his fate is left deliberately in doubt. Can anything be inferred about the kind of man he is? How different might things have been if he had gone with Sethe to 124 Bluestone Road? To put it another way, how important to the story is the fact of his absence?

15) The final chapter suggests a new beginning for Sethe, Denver and Paul D. How do you imagine their lives continuing? Is there good reason to be optimistic?

Suggestions for further reading

Frederick Douglass, *The Narrative of Frederick Douglass, an American Slave*; W.E.B. DuBois, *The Souls of Black Folk*; Louise Erdrich, *Love Medicine*; Euripides, *Medea*; Zora Neale Hurston, *Their Eyes were Watching God*; John Irving, *The Cider House Rules*; Harriet Jacobs, *Incidents in the Life of a Slave Girl*; Edgar Allan Poe, *Tales of Mystery and Imagination*; Harriet Beecher Stowe, *Uncle Tom's Cabin*, *Dred*; Mark Twain, *The Adventures of Huckleberry Finn*; Alice Walker, *The Color Purple*; Harriet Wilson, *Our Nig*; Virginia Woolf, *The Waves*.

Also by Toni Morrison

Fiction: *The Bluest Eye*; *Sula*; *Song of Solomon*; *Tar Baby*; *Jazz*

Non-fiction: *Playing in the Dark*; *Birth of a Nation-hood* herself to that consciously or unconsciously. On the other hand, they can resist being that reader.

ACTIVITY 18

Describe the implied reader of these two novel openings.

Novel A

1 Wanda, Scarlet and Byzantia

Down among the women. What a place to be! Yet here we all are by accident of birth, sprouted breasts and bellies, as cyclical of nature as our timekeeper the moon – and down here among the women we have no option but to stay. So says Scarlet's mother Wanda, aged sixty-four, gritting her teeth.

On good afternoons I take the children to the park. I sit on a wooden bench while they play on the swings, or roll over and over down the hill, or mob their yet more infant victims – disporting in dog mess and inhaling the swirling vapours that compose our city air.

The children look healthy enough, says Scarlet, Wanda's brutal daughter, my friend, when I complain.

Novel B

Chapter One The Worst Birthday

Not for the first time, an argument had broken out over breakfast at number four, Privet Drive. Mr Vernon Dursley had been woken in the early hours of the morning by a loud, hooting noise from his nephew Harry's room.

'Third time this week!' he roared across the table. 'If you can't control that owl, it'll have to go!'

Harry tried, yet again, to explain.

'She's bored,' he said. 'She's used to flying around outside. If I could just let her out at night.'

'Do I look stupid?' snarled Uncle Vernon, a bit of fried egg dangling from his bushy moustache. 'I know what'll happen if that owl's let out.'

COMMENTARY

Novel A opens in a dramatic style using the present tense and the immediacy of a colloquial voice to position the reader in an intimate relationship with the narrator. The identity of the narrator is not made clear and the narrative does not use speech marks for the other speakers so it assumes an effect like a chorus, merging characters, narrator and reader in one voice. We are drawn into this group. The implied reader is female and disillusioned, sharing the narrator's cynical view of contemporary life ('the swirling vapours') and of the position of women. This is taken from *Down Among the Women* by Fay Weldon, written at a time (beginning of the 1970s) when the second phase of the feminist movement was becoming strong. Of course, you may be a male real reader; how would you relate to the implied reader here?

Novel B was originally written for children; it is the second of J. K. Rowling's *Harry Potter* novels. The chapter title perhaps signals the implied reader as a child, which is reinforced by the sympathetic position the reader occupies in relation to the boy whose Uncle is a bully, but presented as a comic figure here, obviously stupid compared to Harry. Although the details at the beginning serve to place the situation, many readers will already know them and they also serve as a shortcut for children familiar with the first book. The first Harry Potter was repackaged with a different cover for adults. The books have also been popular with adult readers; does that suggest anything to you about the concept of implied readers? Did you feel the implied reader was male or female or that gender was irrelevant? Although the author is a woman, her publishing company chose to sell her books under the initials J.K. Why do you think this might be?

Putting these approaches to work

The following is a complete short story by the American writer, Jayne Anne Phillips.

Solo Dance

She hadn't been home in a long time. Her father had a cancer operation; she went home. She went to the hospital every other day, sitting for hours beside his bed. She could see him flickering. He was very thin and the skin on his legs was soft and pure like fine paper. She remembered him saying 'I give up' when he was angry or exasperated. Sometimes he said it as a joke, 'Jesus Christ, I give up'. She kept hearing his voice in the words now even though he wasn't saying them. She read his get-well cards aloud to him. One was from her mother's relatives. Well, he said, I don't think they had anything to do with it. He was speaking of his divorce two years ago.

She put lather in a hospital cup and he got up to shave in the mirror. He had to lean on the sink. She combed the back of his head with water and her fingers. His hair was long after six weeks in the hospital, a gray-silver full of shadow and smudge. She helped him get slowly into bed and he lay against the pillows breathing heavily. She sat down again. I can't wait till I get some weight on me, he said. So I can knock down that son-of-a-bitch lawyer right in front of the courthouse.

She sat watching her father. His robe was patterned with tiny horses, sorrels in arabesques. When she was very young, she had started ballet lessons. At the first class her teacher raised her leg until her foot was flat against the wall beside her head. He held it there and looked at her. She looked back at him, thinking to herself it didn't hurt and willing her eyes dry.

Her father was twisting his hands. How's your mother? She must be half crazy by now. She wanted to be by herself and brother that's what she got.

ACTIVITY 19

If you are a large group, divide into two smaller working groups.

A One group should work on the short story using the technique of photocopying it and pasting it onto a large sheet of paper. You then work around the text filling in detailed responses. These should include: asking questions, noting reactions, commenting on the language, sentence structure and shape of the text.

B The other group should examine the story using the events, storyline and discourse model of analysis detailed earlier on in this chapter.

When you have finished, present your ideas about the story to each other. If you are working on your own, try both methods and compare them. Ask yourselves which was more productive and if there were still things you felt you had not tackled, or would like to know more about in order to feel you had covered the text fully.

COMMENTARY

The key *events* in this short story are the child's experience of pain at the ballet lesson; the parents' divorce; the father's cancer and the hospital visits. The *storyline* moves backwards and forwards between these events, implying connections between them. The narration does not make explicit these connections; in fact because the *discourse*, the telling of the story, is so minimal and stark, the reader fills in the gaps. The second sentence uses a semi-colon (;) a form of punctuation which is used instead of a full stop where two separate sentences are linked in meaning. The ; carries the link so the reader understands that she only went home because her father had cancer. The first two paragraphs move between the events of the sickness of the father and the marital breakdown; the third between the child's confrontation of pain at ballet and the father's in the hospital. The final short paragraph brings in the mother's isolation.

The shifts in the discourse invite the reader to develop ideas about the relationship of the past and present and the patterns in family history. Although the text is told from the point of view of the daughter, the father's speech is not distinguished by speech marks and so seems a part of her. The only line in speech marks is a line he did not *actually* say, but she remembered him saying. They both remain anonymous, but the pathos of their situation affects the reader through the poetic use of poignant detail in the narration ('She could see him flickering'.) and the contrast between the macho bluster of the father's past and the fragility of his present.

This is a complete short story and works in a condensed, highly concentrated way like a poem, making its meaning through imagery, juxtaposition of sentences and ellipsis (the process whereby the gaps carry meaning). Critics sometimes distinguish between the short story that emphasises events, 'what happens', and stories that have a foreground narration, drawing our attention to how a story is told, which are more 'lyrical' like prose-poems. The title of this lyrical piece is significant, perhaps suggesting that the story has an existentialist meaning, that life itself is a 'solo dance' where we may come to some kind of terms with our own suffering and isolation or we may remain bewildered.

What's missing from the two different approaches you have just tried is a sense of genre and contexts. You may have found, for example, that you wanted to find out more about the form of the short story and in particular the ways American writers in the late twentieth century worked with it and with this minimalist style of realism. The context that you might have considered during these activities was the context of the reader and the ideas you brought to the text. For example, one student who had lived in the US and Canada understood the word 'smudge' in a different way from the rest of the group, as having the connotations of spiritual cleansing associated with the American Indian ritual of smudging.

In this chapter you have examined prose fiction using some analytical ideas from narratology and reception theory (reader-response). Such approaches have had a strong impact on the way novels are studied, but the danger can be that they are ahistorical and do not consider the contexts in which the text was produced. They do help illuminate our understanding of texts and our responses to them but we need to remember that readers and texts do not stand outside of history. Nor do analytical approaches, of course, and we have also seen how what students are expected to look at in novels has changed since the 1960s.

4 The Nineteenth Century Novel: Approaching Realism

In this chapter you will consider in detail the type of prose fiction that is called realism, which has been enormously important in the development of the novel. You will examine the conventions of realism by working on nineteenth century texts.

What is realism?

Realism is a very slippery term. We use words connected with it all the time. For example, what do you understand by the following expressions?

> Let's be realistic about his chances in the race.
> That statue is so realistic.
> This book seems so real to me.
> George Eliot writes realist novels.

'Realist' is often used to refer to a period of novel writing in English Literature, the nineteenth century, sometimes called 'classic realist'. However, it is often used more broadly to describe a type of novel which features characters, settings and events which closely resemble real life. Thus, realist novels could also be written in the twenty-first century. In fact quite a lot of works of fiction, popular as well as 'classic' come into this category.

ACTIVITY 20

In groups, quickly draw up a list of titles you have read between you over the past six months or year. Focus on books you chose to read rather than examination texts. Tell each other about the books and discuss whether you would call them 'realist' novels. Identify together the criteria you used when deciding whether the books were realistic or not.

It may seem a difficult task to pin down the meaning of this term 'realism', but it is essential that, as students of literature, you scrutinise the way it is used when you come across it or when you use it yourselves. Assumptions and expectations about realism underlie our understanding of the novel form in particular. The survey of new students' views on prose (mentioned in Chapter 1) suggested that they expected novels to focus on characters and society and to study their 'message' about 'the human condition'. They were in fact giving a good description of the classic 'realist' novel. At the same time, they did not expect to study 'genre' texts at A level, so they did not consider realism to be a 'type' of text in the same way as, for example, crime or science fiction novels. As they found when they looked at the exam specifications, the texts studied at A level are often either classic realist texts or are interesting because of their relationship to the realist tradition, for example being defined as **magic realism** (see Chapter 7).

Realism in the nineteenth century

In the previous chapter we looked at how accounts of the novel have associated its development with the changing nature of society. That particular argument goes along the lines that the greater concern with the specific and 'real' or empirical world, its social and economic nature and the experience of the individual within it, led to a form of writing in the eighteenth century that could fully convey this: the novel. The critic Roland Barthes in an essay on *The Reality Effect* points out how literary realism coincides with the nineteenth and twentieth century concern to 'authenticate the real: the photograph (immediate witness of "what was there", reportage, exhibitions of ancient objects ... the tourism of monuments and historical sites.' (You might like to think whether this is true of media and culture today.) Photography is an interesting comparison. It was also a form of representation that became established in the early decades of the nineteenth century. If you compare a photograph and a painting of the same scene, which do you feel is more realistic? Why? If someone were to show you their holiday snaps they might say, 'This is a photo of me and my friend trying to do Greek dancing in a taverna.' Or 'This one is of Jack at the bar'. If, however, they showed you their diary with the sentence, 'Last night, Jack and I had a go at dancing in the taverna.' they would be unlikely to add, 'That sentence is a representation of my evening out.' The interesting word is 'of'. We find it easy to recognise the photograph as a representation *of something else*. The frames of the photograph are very visible but language seems so natural to us that the way it frames experience is much harder to see. When we study realist novels, we need to remember that they are a representation and the characters and settings we identify in them are not 'real'. To do this we need to examine the frame and what is put into it.

Narrative conventions: beginnings and endings

ACTIVITY 21

Look at the following sentences, which are taken from the beginnings and endings of nineteenth century novels. Read them quickly and decide with a partner which one is an opening line and which a closing line. Try to match up the first and last lines of the five different books.

1 But, in spite of these deficiencies, the wishes, the hopes, the confidence, the predictions of the small band of true friends who witnessed the ceremony, were fully answered in the perfect happiness of the union.

2 Emma Woodhouse, handsome, clever, and rich, with a comfortable home and happy disposition, seemed to unite some of the best blessings of existence; and had lived nearly twenty-one years in the world with very little to distress or vex her.

3 And side by side they retraced their steps down the grey still valley to Castle Boterel.

4 Miss Brooke had that kind of beauty which seems to be thrown into relief by poor dress.

5 My godmother lived in a handsome house in the clean and ancient town of Bretton. Her husband's family had been resident there for generations, and bore, indeed, the name of their birthplace – Bretton of Bretton.

6 Madame Beck prospered all the days of her life; so did Pere Silas; Madame Walravens fulfilled her ninetieth year before she died. Farewell.

7 I took her hand in mine, and we went out of the ruined place; and, as the morning mists had risen long ago when I first left the forge, so, the evening mists were rising now, and in all the broad expanse of tranquil light they showed to me, I saw no shadow of another parting from her.

8 Elfride Swancourt was a girl whose emotions lay very near the surface.

9 My father's family name being Pirrip, and my christian name Philip, my infant tongue could make of both names nothing longer or more explicit than Pip. So I called myself Pip, and came to be called Pip.

10 But the effect of her being on those around her was incalculably diffusive: for the growing good of the world is partly dependent on unhistoric acts; and that things are not so ill with you and me as they might have been, is half owing to the number who have lived faithfully a hidden life, and rest in unvisited tombs.

Did you find this task easy?

What textual clues prompted your decisions? Was it to do with choice of words (which ones?) or sentence structure or style? Be as specific as possible.

Think about the way we use our voice telling the beginning and the ending of a story. Think of traditional frames for oral tales or children's stories ('Once upon a time' and 'And they all lived happily ever after'). Say these phrases out loud. Then try, for example, reading out 4 as an ending line, imagining closing the book shut at the full stop: *Miss Brooke had that kind of beauty which seems to be thrown into relief by poor dress.*

Now try reading 6 as an opening, as if you were to continue reading from it: *Madame Beck prospered all the days of her life; so did Pere Silas; Madame Walravens fulfilled her ninetieth year before she died. Farewell.*

What do you notice?

Draw up two columns and try to identify 'rules' based on these sentences for starting and finishing a novel. Two rules have already been inserted. Complete the table, giving an example for each rule using the sentences above.

Beginnings	Endings
Sets up potential 'trouble' – e.g.	Sense of resolution – e.g.

COMMENTARY Clearly we bring expectations and assumptions to our reading of all texts, and here of narrative prose in particular. You probably identified the beginnings (2, 4, 5, 8, 9) and endings quite quickly, but found it much harder to pair up the beginning with the ending, unless you were familiar with the text. In trying to pair up, you are likely to have focused on maintaining consistency in the narrative person, assuming that a novel which starts in the first person (I) or third person (he or she) will end that way. Apart from this, you may have pointed out that the endings could finish any of the beginnings.

Text 2 is the opening of Jane Austen's *Emma* and the central character is the starting point for the novel. Our interest is aroused by the word 'seemed', which undermines the confidence of 'handsome, clever and rich' and we start to expect that something will, in fact, 'distress or vex' her. The ending, text 1, again alludes to possible difficulties, 'deficiencies', but this is followed by the confident, affirmative vocabulary of closure: 'true', 'fully', 'perfect'. The sentence reverses and completes the opening sentence. A number of the opening lines began with names – of people and place, whereas several of the closing ones began with a conjunction, 'but' or 'and'. An example here would be 8 which is from Thomas Hardy's novel, *A Pair of Blue Eyes,* finishing with line 3. The imagery here creates a powerful sense of the completion of a journey – a journey that is now known – 'retraced their steps' and an atmosphere of peace. Imagery is also important in 7, which is the ending of Charles Dickens' *Great Expectations.* There is a strong sense of the completion of a cycle here from the 'morning mists' to the 'evening mists' and the day ending. Another natural cycle, life to death, is evoked in the last words of George Eliot's *Middlemarch* (10), 'rest in unvisited tombs'. These images give the reader a sense of closure and by comparing the cycles of nature to the process of the novel, they 'naturalise' the novel form as if it were somehow organic rather than a product. Charles Dickens originally wrote an ending for *Great Expectations,* which did not romantically unite the characters of Pip and Estella. However, he was persuaded to change the ending to make it more satisfactory for his readers. This happier resolution he described as 'as pretty a little piece of writing as I could, and I have no doubt the story will be more acceptable through the alteration'. Charlotte Brontë, who wrote *Villette* (5 and 6) was also urged to give a 'they married and lived happily ever after' ending to her novel, but in fact she appears to dispose of her character Monsieur Paul in a sea storm, just as he is due to return to wedded bliss with the heroine, Lucy. The text lets the reader imagine he survives, if they wish: 'Let them picture union and a happy succeeding life'. The final word in her text is also interesting. 'Farewell' formally closes the relationship with the reader in a way that explicitly acknowledges the novel as an act of communication. The other texts assume a relationship with the reader in a much more implicit way: 'Miss Brooke had that kind of beauty', for example. We are drawn in here as we collude with the fiction: yes, we know what is meant by THAT sort of beauty.

We bring so many ideas about the novel to any reading of it. We need to examine why it is so easy to slip into texts like these, how readily we understand our relationship with them. What we have seen here is that such novels operate by conventions such as the introduction of character or the evocation of a natural shape or journey. If we try to make one of these beginnings an ending or vice versa, or if we try to continue writing from one of the final sentences, we recognise the force of convention. We read novels with an implicit understanding of their *discourse*, the ways novels make meaning.

ACTIVITY 22

The texts for the previous activity were chosen quite randomly from a selection of nineteenth-century fiction.

Choose recently written novels from your library or your own reading and write out the first and last sentences on separate sheets of paper, out of order. Swap with a partner and carry out the same matching and analysis exercise. Talk together about your findings. You may find something very different from the nineteenth century novels.

Character: 'telling' and 'implied readers'

All the examples we looked at above offered us a character in the first words. Clearly character is an extremely central and important convention in realist novels. Writers have a number of possible ways of creating characters. These include:

- telling us about the character through narrative or authorial comment
- showing us the character by describing their actions
- showing us the character through their dialogues and interactions with other characters
- positioning the reader in relation to the character – inviting us to observe them or receive their point of view or have access to their 'thoughts' in some way.

ACTIVITY 23

Let us return to the opening of *Emma* by Jane Austen and read a bit further.

As you read, note the way your ideas about the character of Emma develop. Pick out the comments that present her favourably and pick out the phrases that are more critical.

Discuss your view of her with your partner and try to identify *where that view comes from*.

Emma Woodhouse, handsome, clever, and rich, with a comfortable home and happy disposition, seemed to unite some of the best blessings of existence; and had lived nearly twenty-one years in the world with very little to distress or vex her.

She was the youngest of the two daughters of a most affectionate, indulgent father and had, in consequence of her sister's marriage, been mistress of his house from a very early period. Her mother had died too long ago for her to have more than an indistinct remembrance of her caresses, and her place had been supplied by an excellent woman as governess, who had fallen little short of a mother in affection.

Sixteen years had Miss Taylor been in Mr Woodhouse's family, less as a governess than a friend, very fond of both daughters, but particularly of Emma. Between them it was more the intimacy of sisters. Even before Miss Taylor had ceased to hold the nominal office of governess, the mildness of her temper had hardly allowed her to impose any restraint; and the shadow of authority being now long passed away, they had been living together as friend and friend very mutually attached, and Emma doing just what she liked; highly esteeming Miss Taylor's judgement, but directed chiefly by her own.

The real evils indeed of Emma's situation were the power of having too much her own way, and a disposition to think a little too well of herself; these were the disadvantages which threatened alloy to her many enjoyments. The danger, however, was at present so unperceived, that they did not by any means rank as misfortunes with her.

COMMENTARY The technique that is being used here is that of 'telling'. There is a third person omniscient narrator who 'oversees' Emma; knows about her past and her strengths and weaknesses. We are presented at the beginning with her apparent virtues and good fortune. The word 'seemed' in the first paragraph perhaps makes us aware that this might be questionable, a case of perspective. The second paragraph sets the word 'indulgent' after 'affectionate'. We are introduced to Miss Taylor who slips between the roles of governess, mother and sister to Emma. In fact, the role of governess is 'nominal' and her authority was only a 'shadow'. The end of the third paragraph juxtaposes what could be an approved quality 'highly esteeming Miss Taylor's judgement' with what is not: 'but directed chiefly by her own'. By the final paragraph here, the reader who has picked up the *implicit* criticism has their suspicions confirmed with the *explicit* criticism of the narrator: 'the real evils ... too much her own way', and so on. The reader is now securely aligned with the narrator. Perhaps we should talk instead about the 'implied reader' here, the kind of reader the text assumes (as discussed in Chapter 3). This would here seem to be someone who recognises the importance of wealth and status, but also of rigorous 'education' of a kind Emma has not received. The narrator and reader are not expected to be too severe about this, but rather to regard the situation with wry humour. Jane Austen is famous for her use of irony. Of course you may be a reader who thinks that actually money *is* the only thing that matters in life, but by the end of the last paragraph here you are probably sitting comfortably with the narrator, partly because the text makes you feel you got there by yourself.

We have identified here two formal aspects of this novel's opening: the way the narrative positions the reader and the device of 'telling'. Try applying this analysis to a novel you are studying.

ACTIVITY 24

To think a bit more about the difference between telling and showing, it is useful to translate the novel into a medium which relies on 'showing'. Drama or films usually show rather than tell.

Read through the following extract. It is the script of the opening of a 1996 film version of *Emma*, starring Gwyneth Paltrow as Emma.

SCENE 1 – HIGHBURY

NARRATOR: In a time when one's town was one's town was one's world ... and the actions at a dance excited greater interest than the movement of armies, there lived a young woman, who knew how this world should be runned.

EMMA: The most beautiful thing in the world is a match well made, and a happy marriage to you both.

MRS WESTON: Oh, thank you Emma. Your painting grows more accomplished every day.

EMMA: You are very kind, but it would be all the better if I had practised my drawing more, as you urged me.

MRS WESTON: It's very beautiful.

MR ELTON: I should never take sides against you, Miss Woodhouse, but your friend is right. It is indeed a job well done.

EMMA: The job well done, Mr Elton was yours in performing the ceremony.

MR WOODHOUSE: Must the church be so drafty, Mr Elton? It is very difficult to surrender the soul when one is worried about one's throat.

MR ELTON: Perhaps some tea and cake would revive you, Mr Woodhouse.

MR WOODHOUSE: Miss Taylor! Surely you are not serving cake at your wedding! Far too rich! You put us all at peril. And I am not alone in feeling so. Where is Mr Penning, the apothecary, he will support me.

MRS WESTON: He's over there, Mr Woodhouse, having some cake.

MR WOODHOUSE: What?!

EMMA: I have to take father home, but dear Miss Taylor – Oh, no! You are dear Miss Taylor no more! You are dear Mrs Weston now! And how happy this must make you. Such happiness this brings to all of us.

MRS WESTON: My dear Emma!

In small groups, compare the film treatment with the opening of the book. If possible, watch the opening sequence on video.

How is Emma presented here?

How is a text that 'tells' translated into a text that 'shows'?

Character: 'showing' and narrative technique

The opening of the novel establishes a particular authority for the telling and for the reader. If we take a later section from the novel, we can examine other techniques, such as showing, that construct character. It does not matter if you have not read *Emma*; remember you will be able to apply this sort of analysis to other texts as well. In the following extract from Chapter 27, Emma has attended a social event at the Coles' home, a family of newly-made wealth and social aspirations, but not equal to the inherited wealth and gentry position of Emma's own family. Jane Fairfax is an educated woman but without wealth and destined to be a governess. Harriet is also poor but has been adopted as a friend by Emma who wishes to 'marry her' off into an appropriate position.

ACTIVITY 25

Read through this extract. If you can, photocopy it so you can underline the text in different colours.

Identify where the text:

- presents the narrator's view
- presents Emma's view

- presents speech directly (using speech marks)
- presents speech indirectly (no speech marks).

Also consider how we are invited to regard Emma here and how the different techniques you have underlined position the reader.

EMMA did not repent her condescension in going to the Coles. The visit afforded her many pleasant recollections the next day; and all that she might be supposed to have lost on the side of dignified seclusion, must be amply repaid in the splendour of popularity. She must have delighted the Coles – worthy people, who deserved to be made happy ! – And left a name behind her that would not soon die away.

Perfect happiness, even in memory, is not common; and there were two points on which she was not quite easy. She doubted whether she had not transgressed the duty of woman by woman, in betraying her suspicions of Jane Fairfax's feelings to Frank Churchill. It was hardly right; but it had been so strong an idea, that it would escape her, and his submission to all that she told, was a compliment to her penetration which made it difficult for her to be quite certain that she ought to have held her tongue.

The other circumstance of regret related also to Jane Fairfax; and there she had no doubt. She did unfeignedly and unequivocally regret the inferiority of her own playing and singing. She did most heartily grieve over the idleness of her childhood – and sat down and practised vigorously an hour and a half.

She was then interrupted by Harriet's coming in; and if Harriet's praise could have satisfied her, she might soon have been comforted.

'Oh! if I could but play as well as you and Miss Fairfax!'

'Don't class us together, Harriet. My playing is no more like her's than a lamp is like sunshine.'

'Oh! dear – I think you play the best of the two. I think you play quite as well as she does. I am sure I had much rather hear you. Every body last night said how well you played.'

'Those who knew any thing about it, must have felt the difference. The truth is, Harriet, that my playing is just good enough to be praised, but Jane Fairfax's is much beyond it.'

'Well, I always shall think that you play quite as well as she does, or that if there is any difference nobody would ever find it out. Mr Cole said how much taste you had; and Mr Frank Churchill talked a great deal about your taste, and that he valued taste much more than execution.'

'Ah! but Jane Fairfax has them both, Harriet.'

'Are you sure? I saw she had execution, but I did not know she had any taste. Nobody talked about it. And I hate Italian singing. – There is no understanding a word of it. Besides, if she does play so very well, you know, it is no more than she is obliged to do, because she will have to teach. The Coxes were wondering last night whether she would get into any great family. How did you think the Coxes looked?'

'Just as they always do – very vulgar.'

'They told me something,' said Harriet rather hesitatingly, 'but it is nothing of any consequence.'

Emma was obliged to ask what they had told her, though fearful of its producing Mr Elton.

'They told me – that Mr Martin dined with them last Saturday.'

'Oh!'

'He came to their father upon some business, and he asked him to stay to dinner.'

'Oh!'

'They talked a great deal about him, especially Anne Cox. I do not know what she meant, but she asked me if I thought I should go and stay there again next summer.'

'She meant to be impertinently curious, just as such as Anne Cox should be.'

'She said he was very agreeable the day he dined there. He sat by her at dinner. Miss Nash thinks either of the Coxes would be very glad to marry him.'

'Very likely. – I think they are, without exception, the most vulgar girls in Highbury.'

Harriet had business at Ford's. Emma thought it most prudent to go with her. Another accidental meeting with the Martins was possible, and, in her present state, would be dangerous.

COMMENTARY A number of different strategies present Emma here. The chapter opens in the voice of the narrator. The last sentence of the first paragraph inserts Emma's voice in parenthesis: 'She must have delighted the Coles – worthy people who deserved to be made happy! – And left a name behind her that would not soon die away.' This is indirect speech. Although it has not been attributed, it clearly belongs to the register and attitude the reader associates with the character of Emma. This technique is sometimes called **free indirect speech** or **free indirect discourse** and is regarded as a significant development in the way a novel could present character. Instead of a story being told either in the first person or by a third person onlooker, there are a range of voices and positions occupied in this piece. The reader is doing a lot of work here making sense of this. Emma's direct speech, for example the repeated 'Oh!' invites the reader to infer her meaning. In this case the reader of the novel is aware that Emma does not approve of Mr Martin. When Emma goes to the shop door, the reader observes the community of Highbury through her eyes. The last line of that paragraph, however, 'A mind lively and at ease, can do with seeing nothing, and can see nothing that does not answer', reminds us that Emma's vision which we have been occupying is in fact limited and partial. Emma sees only what suits her.

Setting

So far we have been thinking about this extract in terms of presentation of character, but the use of setting is a very important device in realist novels too. Just as Emma here sees only what she wants to see, setting is created so that readers see what writers want us to see. Highbury, as Emma sees it here, is presented as a very ordered world. It is a small rural community where everyone has a clear place in the social hierarchy. One criticism that is sometimes levelled at Austen's novels is that they ignore the wider political world. The film script of *Emma* we looked at earlier in this chapter made just this point through its narrative voice-over. That casts the film very much as having a retrospective twentieth century framework and implies that the story of *Emma* will be dealing with trivia while the serious business of wars are going on. If you have seen the film you should consider whether it does simply dismiss anything political and if you have read the book you might want to argue against this charge at Jane Austen. The fact that the wars are not a focus does not mean that there is no serious social comment.

ACTIVITY 26

In small groups, imagine you have been asked to prepare the film script of *Emma* and you are working on the part of the text examined above, where Emma and Harriet discuss the visit to the Coles and Jane Fairfax and then visit the village shop, Ford's. It may help to find out a bit more about the time *Emma* was written before you decide what to do with the setting in this task, but it can be done on this passage alone. The year before *Emma* was published, 1815, the English wars against Napoleon were won at Waterloo and the Corn Law meant very high bread prices and much hardship for the poor, at a time when the gentry who might be expected to help the poor were less inclined to take on this responsibility.

Set your script out simply as follows:

DIALOGUE	CAMERA SHOTS
Emma:	
Harriet:	

Write two contrasting versions. The first should offer a sentimental version, which admires Emma and her world. The second should imply a critical view of Emma and her society. When you have finished, talk together about how you did this and the different effects.

Some concluding points

The focus on character was very marked in the novel as it developed in the eighteenth and nineteenth centuries and it is still a key aspect students expect to study today; it remains a central convention of the novel. Many realist novels, such as those by Austen, are centrally engaged with ideas about character *formation*. As we saw in the chapter on the history of the novel, some critics would argue that the entrepreneurs of rising capitalism emphasised a strong sense of social position and self-awareness and that the novel's attention to construction of character served this interest in identity and the morality of fashioning or making an appropriate 'self'.

The nineteenth century writer G.H. Lewes, who was the partner of another very famous writer of realist novels, George Eliot (the pseudonym of Marian Evans), said of Jane Austen: '. . . instead of telling us what her characters are, and what they feel, she presents the people and they reveal themselves'. This is one of the ways in which we are convinced of the 'reality' we are being presented with in these nineteenth century novels. It is, of course, a technique we are very used to and we might feel less comfortable with a text where we were told *what the characters are*. The conventions of realism remain very strong. In fact, so strong that it can be argued that, rather than imitating 'real life', realist novels imitate realist novels. It is also important to consider the dynamic, changing nature of the novel. The realism of the early nineteenth century is not exactly the same as the realism of the early twenty-first century, however much it might draw on its conventions of plot, setting and character. Realism today is, for example, also influenced by media such as television, film and the Internet, all of which are concerned with the representation of 'real life'. Think, for example, about the way 'reality TV' programmes like *Big Brother* or films like *Time Code* made in 2000, use 'realtime' and 'real people'.

In this chapter you have considered some of the conventions and narrative strategies of prose fiction known as realism and some ideas about why this form developed and remains so influential.

5 The Nineteenth Century: Comparing Critical Approaches

I n this chapter you will learn about different theoretical approaches to literary texts and how these might be applied to the study of a nineteenth century text, in this case, *Frankenstein*. You will consider how you might apply such approaches and work on other Gothic texts, including those from the twentieth century.

What is Literary Theory?

One of the assessment objectives for the A level English Literature specification is: 'articulate independent opinions and judgements, informed by different interpretations of literary texts by other readers' (AO4). As students of literature you will be aware that there is no one single meaning to be found in a text, rather there are plural meanings and different readers will find different meanings at different times. This is not the same as saying that you can find whatever you want in a text. Debating interpretations and clarifying your own views are some of the most interesting activities involved in studying English. You may well be encouraged to read some literary criticism and discuss whether you agree or disagree with the interpretations offered. Literary theory means something different from literary criticism. The *theory* or theories (the underlying views on literature and literary study) will shape the *criticism* that a critic writes. You will already have a view of literature, which influences you as a student of literature. This might involve, for example, the belief that studying literature is worthwhile or that it involves close reading of texts in ways that are different from any other sorts of reading. You might like to think where your own views have come from. Studying literature, however much we enjoy it, is not 'natural' but learned in particular ways. We all have a view on what we should be doing when we study literature, but some viewpoints are more obvious than others. Literary *theory* then is not something separate or tacked on; it is what underpins literary criticism. It can, however, sound very daunting and some people talk about it as if it is a subject separate from English Literature.

Some understanding of literary theory is very useful not only for AO4 (the 'interpretations' AO) but also for AO5 ('show understanding of the contexts in which literary texts are written and understood') because the ways we understand texts depend on our theoretical positions, which, like all other contexts, are not fixed. When we study a literary text we study its contexts, where it came from. If we examine a critical essay on a text we also need an understanding of where that came from too, so theory is one of the most important contexts for criticism. Theory also changes over time. Just as we can tell a story of the novel, we can tell a story of literary theory. In fact, the two stories run together quite closely because English Literature is a relatively young subject, just as the novel, as we usually define it, is a relatively young form. Some writers point out that the growth of literary criticism coincides with the ascendance of the novel form in the nineteenth and twentieth centuries and certainly a great many ideas have been debated in connection with prose narrative.

As we noted in Chapter 2, the novel in the nineteenth century was often seen as serving a moral purpose and this tied in with the views of Victorian critics, such as Matthew Arnold, who saw literature as a moralising force. Culture was regarded as 'improving' so English Literature was important not only in the education of people living in England, but also in the colonies, such as India, that were part of the British Empire.

English Literature became established as an academic subject in the Universities in the early part of the twentieth century, particularly after the First World War. The increasing loss of faith in God and the horror of the war experiences perhaps also contributed to a need to believe in a good, humanising force, as Literature was seen to be by very influential critics such as F.R. Leavis. This was one argument for the importance of Literature as a subject. In order to justify its academic status, however, it needed to prove itself as a rigorous form of study, not just a chance to indulge in a good read. Academics at Cambridge such as I.A. Richards and Leavis advanced an approach to English that we often call **practical criticism**, based on thorough close readings of texts. This is still an approach much favoured in English studies in schools and colleges because it focuses entirely on detailed attention to the language and form of texts. It is based on the premise that the meaning is there in the text itself and if the reader is skilled enough and has the 'right' sort of judgment, they will be able to work out the meaning and evaluate the worth or quality of the piece of writing. The Leavis approach we considered in Chapter 2 is rooted in practical criticism and separating the 'great' from the 'second-rate'. Although this remains a widespread attitude, it has been criticised for its elitist values and for the assumption that there can be such a thing as an objective reading of a text. Most particularly its critics point to its lack of interest in anything other than the text, such as the historical and political circumstances of reading and writing.

The twentieth century saw the development of a number of very significant alternative approaches towards literature. The effects of key ideas from the nineteenth century meant that beliefs in 'essentialism' were breaking down. Essentialism is the belief that things are determined. Most significantly it means that certain conditions or traits are seen as fixed, such as 'women are like this because they are female' or that race or skin colour determines your characteristics. It proposes that the human subject is unchanged by historical or cultural contexts. For example, after Darwin's theory of evolution, it was harder to believe in 'essential' ideas about the nature of

God and Man. 'Common sense' ideas that our relationships with the world are straightforward were increasingly challenged by key thinkers. Karl Marx introduced the idea of 'false consciousness' – that our understanding of the world is not natural but based on society. Sigmund Freud's development of psychoanalysis presented the idea of the subconscious mind at work beneath the thoughts we are aware of. Linguists and anthropologists studying societies and languages broke down the notion of a simple relationship between the words we use and what they represent. So ideas that texts (or people) simply *say what they mean* were being undermined from a number of directions. This has had a great influence on the ways literature has been and is studied.

Freud's theories, such as those on the interpretation of dreams, seemed to transfer quite smoothly to the interpretation of literary texts. If you practise a ***psychoanalytic*** approach, you might 'analyse' a character in the way that Freud's theory of the Oedipus complex, whereby the male desires his mother and wishes to displace his father, was famously applied to Shakespeare's Hamlet. However, many critics are not happy with the idea of putting characters 'in the psychiatrist's chair', treating them as real people rather than fictional constructs. Psychoanalytic approaches offer more than this. They were and are interested, not just in the manifest or surface meanings, but in the latent or hidden meanings, the ways texts can twist, displace, hide, avoid or use symbolism. They can focus on the processes at work in the text or processes of meaning in language more generally; they can turn the attention on to the mind of the reader or on to the writer of the text.

If you follow a ***Marxist*** approach to studying literature, you would be concerned with placing texts in their historical and cultural contexts. You would be interested in how the text was produced and the economic and social relationships that determined its productions and its meanings. You would be interested in examining relationships of power and powerlessness at work in and around the text. By doing this you would be investigating ideological processes. **Ideology** is a complex term and is often loosely used, but here it refers to the ways certain conditions or ideas about society (that might be unequal or unfair) come to be regarded as an accepted and 'natural' state of affairs. An example might be the way that cultural beliefs about the intellectual and moral inferiority of black-skinned races were used to make the institution of slavery acceptable.

The influence of linguists and anthropologists who have studied the structures of language led to the development of ***structuralist*** approaches to literature. This was interested in examining the relationship between the signifier (the word JAM for example) and the signified (the sweet fruit preserve in the jar). This is an arbitrary relationship in a way, because we could agree instead to call the sweet preserve FUGGLE. It is the convention of calling it JAM that makes its meaning possible. In the same way, structuralists would be interested in looking at the conventions in texts that make it possible to find meaning in them. Structuralists were not interested in anything outside the text, but focused on analysing its parts and their relationships to each other, as you might label the functions of words in a sentence as verbs, subjects and modifiers, for example, and then describe their positions.

This emphasis on the content of the text is completely different from the emphasis of the *reader response* critics. For them, the meaning of the text is made by the reader and does not simply rest in the text waiting to be picked out. They draw attention to the processes at work in reading and the baggage the reader brings to any reading of any text.

The political movement of *feminism* was enormously influential in the development of literary theory in the second half of the twentieth century. Feminist writers looked at the ways women were represented in texts; they revalued the traditionally male-dominated literary canon and restored forgotten or displaced women writers or constructed alternative matrilineal canons (historical lines of women writers); they examined women's relationships to writing, reading, language and criticism.

Many of these approaches have been influenced by work in other academic disciplines. *Cultural* critics for example build on the work of historians or sociologist or studies of the media. They are as interested in 'popular' culture as in 'high' culture and the ways in which culture is reproduced. They might examine, for example, the popularity of cheaply published gothic tales, or the different film versions of *Frankenstein* in considering Mary Shelley's novel.

 Of course the positions critics occupy when they write about a text are rarely anything like as stark as this. Much of the work in literature in recent decades (sometimes rather loosely talked about as post-structuralism or deconstruction) draws on the insights of a number of different theories. *Cultural materialist* approaches for example are heavily influenced by Marxism but also draw on feminism. You can be a Psychoanalytical Feminist Marxist Eco-critic if you want! (Eco-criticism is concerned with environmental issues).

We've moved a long way from the essentialist model of text and reader, which is represented in the diagram below!

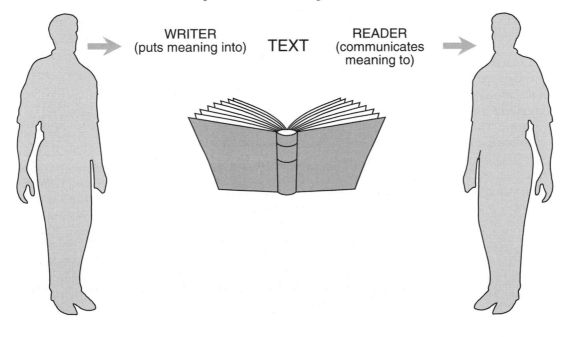

WRITER
(puts meaning into)   TEXT   READER
(communicates
meaning to)

ACTIVITY 27

Get a large sheet of paper. Talk together about what you have just read in this chapter. Working in a group, construct a diagram for a more complex model of factors influencing texts, readers and writers. Make sure it shows the different ideas you have been reading about concerning where meaning is coming from and going to (you could use arrows to show this). If you can, look at an introduction to literary theory such as Robert Eaglestone's *Doing English* to develop your thinking. Add in as many ideas as you can, breaking down the 'big' terms such as *society* or *culture* into more specific factors, for example religion or television. You might want to copy and complete the diagram below or produce your own.

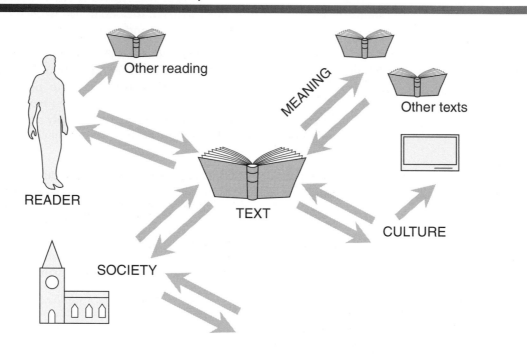

ACTIVITY 28

In the following activity you will try matching up the kinds of questions and the kinds of interpretations that different critical approaches might adopt. The text used as an example here is *Frankenstein*, first published (anonymously) by Mary Shelley in 1818. It is a story almost every English student 'knows' (or thinks they know!) because of the endless ways in which it seems to get 'reproduced'.

The approaches to *Frankenstein* in the following exercise represent the positions that might be adopted by:

A Marxist criticism
B Feminist criticism
C Practical or New criticism – Leavis version
D Psychoanalytical criticism
E Structuralist criticism
F Reader response criticism

In the first column are the questions that might be asked in studying the text and in the second the comments that might be made. Your task is to match these questions (one to six) and statements (i to vi) to a theoretical approach A–F. If you can, photocopy or copy them onto small pieces of card and in groups shuffle them around until you feel happy that you have organised them into their appropriate theoretical approach.

Questions:

ONE
- What do you think this text suggests about the ways men and women behave in the society the text presents?
- In what ways do women feature in this text? How is this different from the male characters?
- Is the position of women a concern of this text?
- Does the text make you see men or women in particular ways?

TWO
- What can you tell about the state of mind of the person who produced this text?
- What does this text suggest about the WRITER and his/her concerns that might be important?
- Are there subjects that the writer avoids or tries to cover up by dealing with them in other ways e.g. through symbols, dreams, the subconscious?
- What four words would you use to specify the feelings the text suggests? Justify from the text.

THREE
- How do you respond to the novel?
- How does the telling of the text, for example the use of the letters as the framework for the text, position you?
- How did you make sense of the relationship between Frankenstein and Walton?

FOUR
- What kind of text is this?
- What conventions does the writer use?
- Give examples of imagery, description and other literary techniques in the text. Are they successful?
- Is this a satisfying text? Do you find it satisfying? Is it a great, flawed or second-rate piece of literature? Justify your view. How do you know?

FIVE
- What do we know about the time in history when this text was written?
- What does the TEXT tell us about the time when this was written?
- Who was the text written for?
- How was the text produced?
- What do we know about reactions to the text at the time of its production?
- What values(beliefs about society) does the text seem to have?

SIX
- Ignore ideas about what the text is about.
- Draw a diagram to show the way the text works.
- What patterns are repeated in the text?
- What striking combinations can you find of events or language in the text?

Comments:

(i)
Frankenstein is a book about what happens when a man tries to have a baby without a woman, a man whose masculine pursuits lead to destruction rather than creation. It explores the collision between the masculine public sphere and the female private or domestic sphere.

(ii)
The text deals with a series of oppositions – light and dark, the sublime and the terrible, beauty and ugliness, life and death, good and evil, creation and destruction and at the centre of it all is something nameless.

(iii)
Frankenstein is a criticism of the industrial and capitalist revolution and its excesses – it shows machinery and technology out of control in the hands of a man interested in individual advancement. It depicts the awful results of a society that has ceased to care.

(iv)
As you settle into the text, you find yourself being addressed, like Walton's sister, as the sympathetic but remote recipient of this young man's idealism.

(v)
Frankenstein is about Mary Shelley's own life: it is a criticism of her husband, and is based on her own feelings of anger and loss (of mother and baby): no wonder that in Frankenstein, sex is always associated with death and guilt.

(vi)
Frankenstein is basically a horror story, the fantasy of an adolescent girl and not a great piece of literature: it is in many places badly written and had to be improved by her husband, the poet Shelley.

You may have found that your group disputed where to place some of the comments. That is the idea here! Theoretical positions often do overlap, and textual evidence can of course be used in very many ways. You will very likely have argued your case in interesting ways. At the end of the chapter you will find suggestions as to how the questions, comments and quotations could be grouped.

ACTIVITY 29

Now read the following extract from the novel. It is describing Frankenstein's preparation leading up to the creation of the creature. This time, each group should adopt one of the critical positions A–F and discuss how to make a relevant point about the passage based on that view, **supported with a quotation from the extract**. Talk together about the best way to express your point and then write it as a mini paragraph and compare your results. If you know the novel you could select your own passage to work with.

An alternative to this activity would be to apply the sets of questions one to six from the exercise on Frankenstein to a set text you know well. This is best done in small groups, each taking responsibility for a different interpretation.

Compile a series of statements expressing different possible interpretations of that text. Find evidence from the text that you might advance in support of your position.

As a whole class, debate these views.

Extract from *Frankenstein:*

No one can conceive the variety of feelings which bore me onwards, like a hurricane in the first enthusiasm of success. Life and death appeared to me ideal bounds, which I should first break through, and pour a torrent of light into our dark world. A new species would bless me as its creator and source; many happy and excellent natures would owe their being to me. No father could claim the gratitude of his child so completely as I should deserve theirs. Pursuing these reflections, I thought that if I could bestow animation upon lifeless matter, I might in process of time (although I now found it impossible) renew life where death had apparently devoted the body to corruption.

These thoughts supported my spirits, while I pursued my undertaking with unremitting ardour. My cheek had grown pale with study, and my person had become emaciated with confinement. Sometimes, on the very brink of certainty I failed; yet still I clung to the hope which the next day or the next hour might realise. One secret which I alone possessed was the hope to which I had dedicated myself; and the moon gazed on my midnight labours, while with unrelaxed and breathless eagerness, I pursued nature to her hiding places. Who shall conceive the horrors of my secret toil as I dabbled among the unhallowed damps of the grave or tortured the living animal to animate the lifeless clay? My limbs now tremble, and my eyes swim with the remembrance; but then a resistless and almost frantic impulse urged me forward; I seemed to have lost all soul or sensation but for this one pursuit. It was indeed but a passing trance, that only made me feel with renewed acuteness as soon as, the unnatural stimulus ceasing to operate, I had returned to my old habits. I collected bones from charnel houses and disturbed, with profane fingers, the tremendous secrets of the human frame. In a solitary chamber, or rather cell, at the top of the house, and separated from all the other apartments by a gallery and staircase, I kept my workshop of filthy creation; my eyeballs were starting from their sockets in attending to the details of my employment. The dissecting room and the slaughterhouse furnished many of my materials; and often did my human nature turn with loathing from my occupation, whilst, still urged on by an eagerness which perpetually increased, I brought my work near to a conclusion.

For the purposes of this exercise, it was necessary to simplify approaches or reduce them to certain angles rather than others. Many approaches require reading that goes beyond the text itself and would be interested in placing Frankenstein in relation to other texts, literary and non-literary. For reasons of space it has not been possible to do this here. Many such critics from a variety of different theoretical backgrounds would consider the text as an example of **Gothic**, a genre that flourished at the end of the 1700s and was particularly popular with women writers and readers. It is also important to point out that there are other approaches you could usefully investigate. Cultural critics might focus on the many reproductions of this text, such as in films, cartoons or popular fiction. They might analyse how the famous 1931 film version directed by James Whale draws upon the ideas and concerns of the 1920s as well as the technological developments in film-making and compare them to, say, the 1994 version by Kenneth Branagh. **Postcolonial** criticism, on the other hand, might look at the way concerns about the 'other' are constructed at a time when the ethics of slavery were being debated or, for example, the way in which the notion of the unleashed monster was used in parliament as a description of the problem of the colonised Irish.

The conventions of the **Gothic** novel that Mary Shelley drew on for *Frankenstein* are quite different from those of the realist novels that Jane Austen was writing at the same time and which we looked at in the last chapter. Some critics have regarded Gothic as rather tasteless or as inferior to classic realism; others have been interested in it because of the marginal or alternative position it occupies in relation to 'classic' fiction. Because it was often written and read by women, it is a very interesting genre for writers from a feminist perspective and cultural critics have focused on its conventions, popularity and reproduction, particularly in other media such as film. Psychoanalytical approaches examine the ways Gothic can explore taboo and fantasy ideas. Although it can be located in a particular historical period, Gothic, like other fictional conventions, is often revisited and revised. Gothic has flourished towards the ends of centuries (its heyday was the 1790s), perhaps reflecting anxieties about thresholds, borders, continuity and change.

The Smell

There is a room in my house that for reasons of my own I have always kept locked. It is a downstairs room and was once, I imagine, a dining room, though I use it now to store boxes containing items pertaining to my work. It has a large fireplace and windows facing the wall that surrounds my property. These windows are kept shuttered, and the few pieces of furniture in the room are covered with sheets. Every few months I light a fire in the grate, but not this year, for the winter was mild. We observed Christmas with the solemnity appropriate to the holiday, and my wife prepared a festive meal. I do not permit decorations as they tend in my opinion to trivialize the occasion, though I do allow the exchanging of gifts as this nurtures selflessness, provided of course that the gifts are either useful or educational, good books for example.

For I have a family, I have a wife and children. There's also my wife's younger sister living in the house, rather a disorganized young woman I'm afraid. I support these people through my work at the museum, work that demands my utter concentration, and this is why I insist on silence in the house during the early hours of the evening (five to seven). The children are permitted to make conversation at the dinner table provided that it's of a serious nature, and the same applies to my wife (and her sister). A stern regime, you may think, but I point out to you that such was the climate of my father's house, and I have not suffered as a result, the reverse in fact. You will understand my recent consternation, then, when having refused to allow the children to keep a stray dog they'd found and begun to care for, several of them expressed feelings of resentment. What's more, my wife supported them, and so, apparently, did her sister!

I punished them of course. And having punished them I explained to them why I had punished them, though whether they appreciated this I cannot say. And it was a few days after this that I first detected the smell.

Now what is so curious about all this is that the work I do is the sort that appeals to scholarly, even pedantic minds, and requires little in the way of imagination. In my field an inexhaustible passion for small detail is of much greater value than imagination per se, for it is with fragments that I work, incomplete pieces of ancient figures that must be identified and catalogued. Given, then, that this is the type of mind I have, does it not strike you as peculiar that I and I alone should have detected the odor?

Actually it began less as a smell, more a sort of ineffable vague suggestion of sweetness in the air. I suspected at first some uncleanness in the kitchen, and had my wife's sister thoroughly scour the floors, ovens, cupboards, and pantry with carbolic. To no avail. It grew stronger. I had my wife's sister then scrub out all of the downstairs rooms, with the exception of course of the one I keep locked at all times (for reasons of my own), for who could have entered that room, shuttered as it is and I in sole possession of the key? I began, when this scouring failed to eliminate the corruption, to suspect that she herself might be responsible for the smell, in retaliation, perhaps, for what she perceived as the injustice of my position regarding the stray dog; and I interviewed her in my room. She did not respond to my inquiries with candor, and I punished her again. *And the smell grew worse!*

The smell grew worse. It made me think of fruit, ripe fruit – a bowl of plums all gone soft and rotten and turning to slime. Was it any wonder that I began to spend so much time at the museum? Of course I did, I couldn't be in the house with that smell, though what really disturbed me was this: the rest of them pretended it wasn't there. They stared at me blankly when I referred to it. They affected concern, or perplexity, or impatience or boredom or fear, but they pretended it wasn't there. And refer to it I certainly did, how could I not, how could I ignore it, and here's something else that disturbed me, that it came and went, and how do you explain that, its coming and going like that?

My authority began to crumble. The children were not openly insubordinate, rather there was a subtle hesitation in their manner that I found deeply impertinent. One night I heard them on the roof, and they know they're not allowed on the roof, though when I went out into the garden I couldn't see anyone up there. With my wife it was the same, and with her sister: in fact, my wife's sister grew so bold, one day I discovered her rattling the doorknob of the room I keep locked! If you think the smell's coming from in there, I told her tartly, you're wrong. She gave me a saucy look and walked off.

She would have to be punished. I would have to make an example of her. Behavior like this could not be tolerated, not in a man's own house, not from her, not from any of them. You do see that, don't you? You do see that I had to do it, even though they were my own family and I loved them? You see that love must at times be cruel if it is to rise above the merely sentimental? Is it a loving father who fails to guide and instruct his family, who fails to teach them self-control, who permits them to flaunt his authority with impunity?

I decided to begin with my wife's sister. I asked her to join me in that certain room after dinner. This gave me ample opportunity to prepare for her visit. The day passed with excruciating slowness. I could not concentrate on my work, and left the museum earlier than usual. After dinner, as I rose from my chair, I glanced at her, meaningfully, and went out of the room. A moment later she followed me. I crossed the hall, extracting from my trouser pocket the key. I unlocked the door and ushered her in, and at that moment, to my unutterable horror, I discovered that the foulness that had been so tormenting my senses did originate in the locked room after all: it *stank* in there, my God it stank, such a sick, sweet stink that I felt my gorge rise and a wave of nausea almost overwhelmed me. I mastered myself, with some difficulty – and then became aware of something else in the room, some new abomination. It was liquid, dripping liquid, there was a sweet and viscous liquid dripping into the fireplace.

Oh, viscosity! She turned to me and asked why I'd brought her here. She appeared *not to smell the smell*. A light, cold prickle of sweat broke out on my skin and I was barely able to control the impulse to retch though I did control it, I did. She asked me again why I'd brought her here, and again I could not answer, for I'd clapped my hands to my mouth to keep from vomiting.

I stared wildly about me. Boxes of fragments, sheeted chairs, shuttered windows, all swam before my eyes. I told her to go, and as she left the room she barely troubled to conceal her contempt. I managed to lock the door from the inside, and then with no little trepidation I approached the fireplace. I was trembling I remember, and damp with perspiration. I knelt down on the hearth, and careful to avoid the puddle of sticky liquid in the grate leaned forward into the fireplace, turning my head so as to gaze up the chimney. I found only blackness, but the smell was bad, oh, it was very bad indeed, and there was little doubt in my mind that I had discovered the source: somewhere up this chimney, somewhere not far above my head, was the thing that dripped and stank.

In a sudden frenzy of rage and frustration I seized up a broomhandle, intending to dislodge the foulness. But broomhandles are stiff, and as the flue sloped backward at an angle just above the fireplace I was unable to get it to go up. I introduced instead a length of wire, and with this succeeded in negotiating the slope, and then thrust upward forcefully a number of times. All that came down was a shower of dead leaves and soot. I waited a few moments and then tried again. I inserted the wire and pushed and thrust with great violence, but again my efforts availed me nothing but chimney rubbish and coal dust.

I spent the next hours in the room. I paced the floor, pondering the events of the evening. And what I couldn't get out of my mind was the way my wife's sister had looked at me, the way she's spoken to me – it infuriated me, the picture of her flouncing out like that, with a sneer on her lips. That sneer – ! But it wasn't only her, they were all in on it, every single one of them, and I knew that I couldn't delay it much longer, for the situation was rapidly getting out of hand.

They were alarmed now. They knew they'd gone too far. My wife was most agitated when I sent for her, she stood before me fidgeting with great unease and was completely unable to meet my eye. I was not easy on her, I was not easy on any of them, why should I be, after what they'd put me through? But despite my anger I didn't raise a finger, I didn't even raise my voice. I spoke, rather, in cool, quiet tones, I told them what I knew, and saw them grow shifty and afraid, for they had thought me a fool, this was clear now, they'd taken me for a fool.

Dead of night, punishment time. I left my room. I listened to the house. Silence. I am a small-boned, agile man, slightly built, simian in fact. I padded quickly and quietly up the stairs, two at a time, and came to the door of my wife's sister's bedroom. I put my ear to the door. I could hear nothing. I crossed the landing and entered another bedroom. A sleeping child sprawled on the bed with sheet and blanket tangled about its limbs. Then I heard coughing, and I went down the passage to a room where two of the younger children slept. I would start here. I went in and closed the door behind me. I was feeling an immense sadness: oh, that it should come to this – two sleeping children – little fragments, delicate, unfinished things, but no less guilty for that. Then the anger came and I experienced the familiar sensation, the *milky* feeling – how else to describe it? – the sudden loss of clarity, the rapid shift into a sort of pale sunless liquid mist, the numbness, watching the horror from somewhere outside one's own body, and when it had passed, when it was over, finding myself once more out in the passage and *again* the sadness, again the intense, almost overwhelming sense of sorrow, though something had changed, for now there was something that was stronger even than the sorrow.

Even from upstairs I could tell it had grown worse, much, much worse. I knew then I *had* to have done with it, that I could wait no longer: more punishment later, I thought, though in an odd way it was no longer me thinking, no longer me in control, for I was drawn to the smell like a moth to a flame, it was *pulling me in*. Rapidly I descended the stairs and unlocked the room – and almost gagged, it was so strong, the wave of foulness that hit me, but in I came, and covering nose and mouth with my arm stumbled to the fireplace and this time ducked my head under the mantelpiece and stood upright in the foul sooty blackness, *I couldn't help myself!* Above my head bricks projected every three feet, it was stepped, so grasping a brick I began blindly to clamber up the inside of the fireplace to the sloping section. There it became more difficult, for the opening was narrow, but I managed to squeeze myself up and along on my front until I reached the passage of the chimney proper, where I somehow turned myself over in the foetid blackness so I could press my back against the one wall of the chimney, get the soles of my shoes hard against the other, legs bent double, and wedged tight like this start poling upward with the wire. But to my horror I'd wedged myself so tight I couldn't move!

I couldn't move. Slowly the blind hysterical compulsion that had seized me faded, slowly I began to understand where I was, and what I'd done. The effort, then, to suppress panic, and terror, and the nausea born of an almost overwhelming stench of putrefying flesh, as a voice inside my own brain whispered, You're suffocating, you're going to die. You're going to die. You're going to die in this putrid chimney. And *then* the thought, So is it *me*? Is it me who makes the smell? Am I the thing that drips and stinks?

Suddenly in my mind's eye I saw my wife's sister, I saw her as she flounced out of my presence, flung out of the room with her eyes flashing and her little chin lifted, like a little white vessel buoyed and swept forward on the current of her own indignation. And then did I hear her laughing? She was outside the door, laughing at me, and at last I saw it, at last I saw the ghastly gallows humor of it all. For I was indeed the source, I the smell, I the thing that dripped and stank. Behind the locked door I could still hear her laughing, while I slowly suffocated, stuffed up my chimney like a dirty cork in a bottle of rancid milk.

The short story above, published in 1991, is by a highly regarded writer of contemporary Gothic, Patrick McGrath.
Read the story and note down your first responses to it. Then read it again.

Read through the following statements about the story which offer a variety of different readings. Discuss as a group which you find most interesting.

1 *The Smell* is a story that explores the effects of patriarchy. Patriarchy is a society headed by men and centred on male power and interests, perpetuated by being handed down through the male line. In the story, the narrator is the ultimate patriarch and his destruction shows the appalling consequences of such a social system. His misogyny (hatred of women) is particularly evident in the way he wants to damage the womb, as represented by the chimney, but he ends up suffocating in it.

2 *The Smell* is completely tasteless, an unpleasant piece of writing which has no place in English Literature.

3 The story explores the devastating effects of repression. The narrator expresses the extreme forces of control that lead to a psychotic state where his view of reality is deeply disturbed, a kind of split personality whose contradictions are conveyed through the contrast of the implied violent abuse and the 'milky' feeling.

4 The story explores fundamental ideas about the operations of power and authority in a society not specifically located, but clearly presented as twentieth century Western, with the narrator expressing the extremes of a Christian, property-based, male-dominating society which he seeks to conserve through his work as a curator, a preserver of history.

5 Written towards the millennium, the story explores concerns about gender, the family, social and psychological breakdown that were prevalent in the fiction of the 1980s and 1990s. Literary texts and popular culture such as TV and film were haunted by extremes such as violence, incest, and serial killers.

6 The central concern of this story is with the notion of the 'other' and the ways that fear of the 'other', such as women, children or outsiders and the consequent obsession with the 'self' lead to breakdown. The story questions our belief in the idea of the self being unified because the subject of the story, the narrator, is profoundly fractured, despite the controlled and coherent self he presents.

7 Unlike the Gothic of the eighteenth century, modern Gothic puts less emphasis on the supernatural and more on the psychological – less the terror *out there*, more the terror *within* or at the very heart of society, such as the family.

David Lodge in his book, *The Art of Fiction* has a chapter on the uncanny which you might like to refer to. He explains the ideas of the structuralist critic, Todorov, on supernatural tales which puts them into three categories:

'the marvellous, in which no rational explanation of the supernatural phenomenon is possible; the uncanny, in which it is; and the fantastic, in which the narrative hesitates undecidably between a natural and supernatural explanation'.

Is this useful for *The Smell*? Would you prefer a 'mixed' or 'other' category to describe it?

In this chapter you have considered the ways that writers from different theoretical perspectives might offer different interpretations of literary texts.

These approaches vary over time and according to the views of literature and its relationships to society and to language held by the critic. In particular you have thought about ways of writing about Gothic texts.

Answers to *Frankenstein* task:

A   five   iii

B   one   i

C   four   vi

D   two   v

E   six   ii

F   three   iv

6 Reading the Twentieth Century: Approaching Modernism

I n this chapter you will examine how ideas and conventions of prose fiction developed in the early part of the twentieth century. You will particularly focus on the significance of contexts in understanding the writing of the time, as well as addressing how these influence interpretations. You will work closely on a complete text, a short story by Katherine Mansfield.

1 'It is well I drew the curtain,' thought I, and I wished fervently he might not discover my hiding-place: nor would John Reed have found it out himself; he was not quick either of vision or conception; but Eliza just put her head in at the door, and said at once: 'She is in the window seat to be sure, Jack.'

And I came out immediately, for I trembled at the idea of being dragged forth by the said Jack.

'What do you want?' I asked with awkward diffidence.

'Say, 'What do you want, Master Reed,' was the answer. 'I want you to come here;' and seating himself in an armchair, he intimated by a gesture that I was to approach and stand before him.

John Reed was a schoolboy of fourteen years old; four years older than I, for I was but ten; large and stout for his age, with a dingy and unwholesome skin; thick lineaments in a spacious visage, heavy limbs and large extremities. He gorged himself habitually at table, which made him bilious, and gave him a dim and bleared eye with flabby cheeks. He ought now to have been at school; but his mamma had taken him home for a month or two, 'on account of his delicate health'. Mr Miles, the master, affirmed that he would do very well if he had fewer cakes and sweetmeats sent him from home; but his mother's heart turned from an opinion so harsh, and inclined rather to the more refined idea that John's sallowness was owing to over-application, and, perhaps, to pining after home.

2 She was dressed in rich materials – satins, and lace, and silks – all of white. Her shoes were white. Some bright jewels sparkled on her neck and on her hands, and some other jewels lay sparkling on the table. Dresses, less splendid than the dress she wore, and half-packed trunks, were scattered about. She had not quite finished dressing, for she had but one shoe on – the other was on the table near her hand – her veil was but half-arranged, her watch and chain were not put on, and some lace for her bosom lay with those trinkets, and with her handkerchief, and glove and some flowers, and a prayer-book, all confusedly heaped about the looking-glass.

It was not in the first few moments that I saw all these things, though I saw more of them in the first moments than might be supposed. But, I saw that everything within my view which ought to be white, had been white long ago, and had lost its lustre, and was faded and yellow. I saw that the bride within the bridal dress had withered like the dress, and like the flowers, and had no brightness left but the brightness of her sunken eyes. I saw that the dress had been put upon the rounded figure of a young woman, and that the figure upon which it now hung loose, had shrunk to skin and bone. Once, I had been taken to see some ghastly waxwork at the fair, representing I know not what impossible personage lying in state. Once, I had been taken to one of our old marsh churches to see a skeleton in the ashes of a rich dress, that had been dug out of a vault under the church pavement. Now, waxwork and skeleton seemed to have dark eyes that moved and looked at me. I should have cried out if I could.

3   Once upon a time and a very good time it was there was a moocow coming down along the road and this moocow that was coming down along the road met a nicens little boy named baby tuckoo....

His father told him that story: his father looked at him through a glass: he had a hairy face.

He was baby tuckoo. The moocow came down the road where Betty Byrne lived: she sold lemon platt.

> O, the wild rose blossoms
> On the little green place.

He sang that song. That was his song.

> O, the green wothe botheth.

When you wet the bed first it is warm then it gets cold. His mother put on the oilsheet. That had the queer smell.

His mother had a nicer smell than his father. She played on the piano the sailor's hornpipe for him to dance. He danced:

> Tralala lala,
> Tralala tralaladdy,
> Tralala lala,
> Tralala lala.

Uncle Charles and Dante clapped. They were older than his father and mother but Uncle Charles was older than Dante.

ACTIVITY 31

To get a taste of the shift in writing styles you will be dealing with here, look carefully at the above extracts. All of them represent the experiences of a young child and they all use first person narration. All could perhaps be classified as 'bildung' novels (see page 9), which are about the education and character formation of the central character, the protagonist.

The first extract is from Charlotte Bronte's *Jane Eyre* (1847). The young orphan Jane is hiding from the bullying relations, the Reeds, that she lives with.

The second extract is a very famous moment in Charles Dickens' *Great Expectations* (1861) when the young Pip, who is telling the story

meets for the first time the awesome figure of Miss Havisham, the woman who has tried to 'freeze' time at the moment when she was jilted on her wedding day.

The final extract is from the beginning of James Joyce's *A Portrait of the Artist as a Young Man* (1916).

Discuss in pairs the techniques the writers have used to offer the perspective of a child. Think about the language and syntax (sentence structure) they use as well as the way the texts position the reader and the effect they have on the reader. How convincing do you find them? Which do you prefer? Why?

COMMENTARY

We are told that the narrator in *Jane Eyre* is ten years of age, yet the narration is remarkably sophisticated. For example, it invites the reader to adopt an ironic view of her aunt's blind indulgence of her son, John, as she interprets his greed as 'over-application' or 'pining for home'. The narrator is also somehow aware that John is considered spoilt, a view which is held by a teacher at his male boarding school. *Jane Eyre* is a novel that presents itself as an 'autobiography', rather like some of the eighteenth century novels we looked at in Chapter 2 and the narrator, Jane, here occupies several positions: the child of ten feeling the experience; the adult Jane looking back and retelling it and a sort of implied omniscient (all-knowing) narrator who can access information that neither young Jane nor older Jane would be likely to have.

The extract from Dickens's novel also has the double perspective of the child Pip and the adult Pip relating his story. The paragraphing and sentence structure here help to represent the sense both of a 'double-take' and the child's attempt to come to terms with what he sees. Pip's first thought is that he sees wedding preparations. The second paragraph revisits the scene as its true ghastliness becomes clear to him, his awe conveyed in the sweeping movement round the room. The young Pip struggles to make sense of this and tries to relate it to his childhood fears and experiences ('waxwork at the fair'). The adult Pip, narrating the story, understands the implications but puts the reader in the child's position.

The extract from Joyce does not have the authoritative narration that allows the reader to have the adult's clarity and overview. This is a very different piece of writing and may have provoked more questions as you read it. The reader receives all the sensual experiences of a young child and is put in that position where consciousness, awareness of self and others, and understanding of language is developing. The text is very fragmented as it conveys sense impressions. The reader *may* assume that the first voice we encounter is the father's talking to the little boy, and *maybe* he is drinking, holding a 'glass', but the narration does not help us by 'making sense' in the way that the extracts from the nineteenth century novels did, such as using speech marks. The reader may find this text incoherent compared to the realist texts. On the other hand, they may feel this has a 'psychological truth' about a child's experience that the others do not. Nearly a century later, Joyce's text still seems very 'unconventional' to many readers. Modernist writers, such as Joyce, set themselves against the conventions of realism. You will find out more about **modernism** later in this chapter.

The Man Without a Temperament

ACTIVITY 32

Now read the text below. This is a complete short story by Katherine Mansfield called **The Man Without a Temperament**, which was written at the beginning of 1920. When you have completed your first reading of the story, you should discuss your responses to it with a partner.

When you have read the text, respond to the questions below. Did you find the story easy to follow? If it presented difficulties, what were they and how did you resolve them?

Think about and discuss together the ways the characters and the relationships between them are presented in the story. Consider not just the central couple but also the other 'residents' at the hotel, the 'servants' and the 'natives'.

What different societies or social worlds are depicted in the story?

What are the most striking features of the narrative style?

Now using reference books, encyclopaedias or the internet, find out as much as you can about:

■ the life and work of the writer, Katherine Mansfield

■ the historical circumstances around 1920, including key events and changing attitudes
■ and the literary movement of modernism.

Pool your research.

Does what you have found out change or develop your understanding and interpretations of the story?

He stood at the hall door turning the ring, turning the heavy signet ring upon his little finger while his glance travelled coolly, deliberately, over the round tables and basket chairs scattered about the glassed-in veranda. He pursed his lips – he might have been going to whistle – but he did not whistle – only turned the ring – turned the ring on his pink, freshly washed hands.

Over in the corner sat The Two Topknots, drinking a decoction they always drank at this hour – something whitish, greyish, in glasses, with little husks floating on the top – and rooting in a tin full of paper shavings for pieces of speckled biscuit, which they broke, dropped into the glasses and fished for with spoons. Their two coils of knitting, like two snakes, slumbered beside the tray.

The American Woman sat where she always sat against the glass wall, in the shadow of a great creeping thing with wide open purple eyes that pressed – that flattened itself against the glass, hungrily watching her. And she knoo it was there – she knoo it was looking at her just that way. She played up to it; she gave herself little airs. Sometimes she even pointed at it, crying: 'Isn't that the most terrible thing you've ever seen! Isn't that ghoulish!' It was on the other side of the veranda, after all ... and besides it couldn't touch her, could it, Klaymongso? She was an American Woman, wasn't she, Klaymongso, and she'd just go right away to her Consul. Klaymongso, curled in her lap, with her torn antique brocade bag, a grubby handkerchief, and a pile of letters from home on top of him, sneezed for reply.

The other tables were empty. A glance passed between the American and the Topknots. She gave a foreign little shrug; they waved an understanding biscuit. But he saw nothing. Now he was still, now from his eyes you saw he listened. 'Hoo-e-zip-zoo-oo!' sounded the lift. The iron cage clanged open. Light dragging steps sounded across the hall, coming towards him. A hand, like a leaf, fell on his shoulder. A soft voice said: 'Let's go and sit over there – where we can see the drive. The trees are so lovely.' And he moved forward with the hand still on his shoulder, and the light, dragging steps beside his. He pulled out a chair and she sank into it, slowly, leaning her head against the back, her arms falling along the sides.

'Won't you bring the other up closer? It's such miles away.' But he did not move.

'Where's your shawl?' he asked.

'Oh!' She gave a little groan of dismay. 'How silly I am, I've left it upstairs on the bed. Never mind. Please don't go for it. I shan't want it, I know I shan't.'

'You'd better have it.' And he turned and swiftly crossed the veranda into the dim hall with its scarlet plush and gilt furniture – conjuror's furniture – its Notice of Services at the English Church, its green baize board with the unclaimed letters climbing the black lattice, huge 'Presentation' clock that struck the hours at the half-hours, bundles of sticks and umbrellas and sunshades in the clasp of a brown wooden bear, past the two crippled palms, two ancient beggars at the foot of the staircase, up the marble stairs three at a time, past the life-size group on the landing of two stout peasant children with their marble pinnies full of marble grapes, and along the corridor, with its piled-up wreckage of old tin boxes, leather trunks, canvas holdalls, to their room.

The servant girl was in their room, singing loudly while she emptied soapy water into a pail. The windows were open wide, the shutters put back, and the light glared in. She had thrown the carpets and the big white pillows over the balcony rails; the nets were looped up from the beds; on the writing-table there stood a pan of fluff and match-ends. When she saw him her small impudent eyes snapped and her singing changed to humming. But he gave no sign. His eyes searched the glaring room. Where the devil was the shawl!

'*Vous desirez, monsieur*?' mocked the servant girl.

No answer. He had seen it. He strode across the room, grabbed the grey cobweb and went out, banging the door. The servant girl's voice at its loudest and shrillest followed him along the corridor.

'Oh, there you are. What happened? What kept you? The tea's here, you see. I've just sent Antonio off for the hot water. Isn't it extraordinary? I must have told him about it sixty times at least, and still he doesn't bring it. Thank you. That's very nice. One does just feel the air when one bends forward.'

'Thanks.' He took his tea and sat down in the other chair. 'No, nothing to eat.'

'Oh do! Just one, you had so little at lunch and it's hours before dinner.'

Her shawl dropped off as she bent forward to hand him the biscuits. He took one and put in his saucer.

'Oh, those trees along the drive,' she said. 'I could look at them for ever. They are like the most exquisite huge ferns. And you see that one with the grey-silver bark and the clusters of cream-coloured flowers, I pulled down a head of them yesterday to smell, and the scent' – she shut her eyes at the memory and her voice thinned away, faint, airy – 'was like freshly ground nutmegs.' A little pause. She turned to him and smiled. 'You do know what nutmegs smell like – do you, Robert?'

And he smiled back at her. 'Now how am I going to prove to you that I do?'

Back came Antonio with not only the hot water – with letters on a salver and three rolls of paper.

'Oh, the post! Oh, how lovely! Oh, Robert, they mustn't be all for you! Have they just come, Antonio?' Her thin hands flew up and hovered over the letters that Antonio offered her, bending forward.

'Just this moment, Signora,' grinned Antonio. 'I took-a them from the postman myself. I made-a the postman give them for me.'

'Noble Antonio!' laughed she. 'There – those are mine, Robert; the rest are yours.'

Antonio wheeled sharply, stiffened, the grin went out of his face. His striped linen jacket and his flat gleaming fringe made him look like a wooden doll.

Mr Salesby put the letters into his pocket; the papers lay on the table. He turned the ring, turned the signet ring on his little finger and stared in front of him, blinking, vacant.

But she – with her teacup in one hand, the sheets of thin paper in the other, her head tilted back, her lips open, a brush of bright colour on her cheek-bones, sipped, sipped, drank . . . drank . . .

'From Lottie,' came her soft murmur. 'Poor dear . . . such trouble . . . left foot. She thought . . . neuritis . . . Doctor Blyth . . . flat foot . . . massage. So many robins this year . . . maid most satisfactory . . . Indian Colonel . . . every grain of rice separate . . . very heavy fall of snow.' And her wide lighted eyes looked up from the letter. 'Snow, Robert! Think of it!' And she touched the little dark violets pinned on her thin bosom and went back to the letter.

. . . Snow. Snow in London. Millie with the early morning cup of tea. 'There's been a terrible fall of snow in the night, sir.' 'Oh, has there, Millie?' The curtains ring apart, letting in the pale reluctant light. He raises himself in the bed; he catches a glimpse of the solid houses opposite framed in white, of their window boxes full of great sprays of white coral . . . In the bathroom – overlooking the back garden. Snow – heavy snow over everything. The lawn is covered with a wavy pattern of cat's-paws; there is a thick, thick icing on the garden table; the withered pods of the laburnum tree are white tassels; only here and there in the ivy is a dark leaf showing . . . Warming his back at the dining-room fire, the paper drying over a chair. Millie with the bacon. 'Oh, if you please, sir, there's two little boys come as will do the steps and front for a shilling, shall I let them?' . . . And then flying lightly, lightly down the stairs – Jinnie. 'Oh, Robert, isn't it wonderful! Oh, what a pity it has to melt. Where's the pussy-wee?' 'I'll get him from Millie.' . . . 'Millie, you might just hand me up the kitten if you've got him down there.' 'Very good, sir.' He feels the little beating heart under his hand. 'Come on, old chap, your missus wants you.' 'Oh, Robert, do show him the snow – his first snow. Shall I open the window and give him a little piece on his paw to hold? . . .'

'Well, that's very satisfactory on the whole – very. Poor Lottie! Darling Anne! How I only wish I could send them something of this,' she cried, waving her letters at the brilliant, dazzling garden. 'More tea, Robert? Robert dear, more tea?'

'No, thanks, no. It was very good,' he drawled.

'Well, mine wasn't. Mine was just like chopped hay. Oh, here comes the Honeymoon Couple.'

Half striding, half running, carrying a basket between them and rods and lines, they came up the drive, up the shallow steps.

'My! Have you been out fishing?' cried the American Woman.

They were out of breath, they panted: 'Yes, yes, we have been out in a little boat all day. We have caught seven. Four are good to eat. But three we shall give away. To the children.'

Mrs Salesby turned her chair to look; the Topknots laid the snakes down. They were a very dark young couple – black hair, olive skin, brilliant eyes and teeth. He was dressed 'English Fashion' in a flannel jacket, white trousers and shoes. Round his neck he wore a silk scarf; his head, with his hair brushed back, was bare. And he kept mopping his forehead, rubbing his hands with a brilliant handkerchief. Her white skin had a patch of wet; her neck and throat were stained a deep pink. When she lifted her arms big half-hoops of perspiration showed under her arm-pits; her hair clung in wet curls to her cheeks. She looked as though her young husband had been dipping her in the sea and fishing her out again to dry in the sun and then – in with her again – all day.

'Would Klaymongso like a fish?' they cried. Their laughing voices charged with excitement beat against the glassed-in veranda like birds and a strange, saltish smell came from the basket.

'You will sleep well tonight,' said a Topknot, picking her ear with a knitting needle while the other Topknot smiled and nodded.

The Honeymoon Couple looked at each other. A great wave seemed to go over them. They gasped, gulped, staggered a little and then came up laughing – laughing.

'We cannot go upstairs, we are too tired. We must have tea just as we are. Here – coffee. No – tea. No – coffee. Tea – coffee, Antonio!' Mrs Salesby turned.

'Robert! Robert!' Where was he? He wasn't there. Oh, there he was at the other end of the veranda, with his back turned, smoking a cigarette. 'Robert, shall we go for our little turn?'

'Right.' He stumped the cigarette into an ash-tray and sauntered over, his eyes on the ground. 'Will you be warm enough?'

'Oh, quite.'

'Sure?'

'Well,' she put her hand on his arm, 'perhaps' – and gave his arm the faintest pressure – 'it's not upstairs, it's only in the hall – perhaps you'd get me my cape. Hanging up.'

He came back with it and he bent her small head while he dropped it on her shoulders. Then, very stiff, he offered her his arm. She bowed sweetly to the people on the veranda while he just covered a yawn, and they went down the steps together.

'*Vous avez voo ça!*' said the American Woman.

'He is not a man,' said the Two Topknots, 'he is an ox. I say to my sister in the morning and at night when we are in bed, I tell her – *No* man is he, but an ox!'

Wheeling, tumbling, swooping, the laughter of the Honeymoon Couple dashed against the glass of the veranda.

The sun was still high. Every leaf, every flower in the garden lay open, motionless, as if exhausted, and a sweet, rich, rank smell filled the quivering air. Out of the thick, fleshy leaves of a cactus there rose an aloe stem loaded with pale flowers that looked as though they had been cut out of butter; light flashed upon the lifted spears of the palms; over the bed of scarlet waxen flowers some big black insects 'zoom-zoomed'; a great, gaudy creeper, orange splashed with jet, sprawled against a wall.

'I don't need my cape after all,' said she. 'It's really too warm.' So he took it off and carried it over his arm. 'Let us go down this path here. I feel so well today – marvellously better. Good heavens – look at those children! And to think it's November!'

In a corner of the garden there were two brimming tubs of water. Three little girls, having thoughtfully taken off their drawers and hung them on a bush, their skirts clasped to their waists, were standing in the tubs and tramping up and down. They screamed, their hair fell over their faces, they splashed one another. But suddenly, the smallest, who had a tub to herself, glanced up and saw who was looking. For a moment she seemed overcome with terror, then clumsily she struggled and strained out of her tub, and still holding her clothes above her waist, 'The Englishman! The Englishman!' she shrieked and fled away to hide. Shrieking and screaming the other two followed her. In a moment they were gone; in a moment there was nothing but the two brimming tubs and their little drawers on the bush.

'How – very – extraordinary!' said she. 'What made them so frightened? Surely they were much too young to . . .' She looked up at him. She thought he looked pale – but wonderfully handsome with that great tropical tree behind him with its long, spiked thorns.

For a moment he did not answer. Then he met her glance, and smiling his slow smile, '*Très* rum!' said he.

Très rum! Oh, she felt quite faint. Oh, why should she love him so much just because he said a thing like that. *Très* rum! That was Robert all over. Nobody else but Robert could ever say such a thing. To be so wonderful, so brilliant, so learned, and then to say in that queer, boyish voice . . . she could have wept.

'You know you're very absurd, sometimes,' said she.

'I am,' he answered. And they walked on.

But she was tired. She had had enough. She did not want to walk any more.

'Leave me here and go for a little constitutional, won't you? I'll be in one of these long chairs. What a good thing you've got my cape; you won't have to go upstairs for a rug. Thank you, Robert, I shall look at that delicious heliotrope. . . . You won't be gone long?'

'No – no. You don't mind being left?'

'Silly! I want you to go. I can't expect you to drag after your invalid wife every minute. . . . How long will you be?'

He took out his watch. 'It's just after half-past four. I'll be back at a quarter-past five.'

'Back at a quarter-past five,' she repeated, and she lay still in the long chair and folded her hands.

He turned away. Suddenly he was back again. 'Look here, would you like my watch?' And he dangled it before her.

'Oh!' She caught her breath. 'Very, very much.' And she clasped the watch, the warm watch, the darling watch in her fingers. 'Now go quickly.'

The gates of the Pension Villa Excelsior were open wide, jammed open against some bold geraniums. Stooping a little, staring straight ahead, walking swiftly, he passed through them and began climbing the hill that wound behind the town like a great rope looping the villas together. The dust lay thick. A carriage came bowling along driving towards the Excelsior. In it sat the General and the Countess; they had been for his daily airing. Mr Salesby stepped to one side but the dust beat up, thick, white, stifling like wool. The Countess just had time to nudge the General.

'There he goes,' she said spitefully.

But the General gave a loud caw and refused to look.

'It is the Englishman,' said the driver, turning round and smiling. And the Countess threw up her hands and nodded so amiably that he spat with satisfaction and gave the stumbling horse a cut.

On – on – past the finest villas in the town, magnificent palaces, palaces worth coming any distance to see, past the public gardens with the carved grottoes and statues and stone animals drinking at the fountain, into a poorer quarter. Here the road ran narrow and foul between high lean houses, the ground floors of which were scooped and hollowed into stables and carpenters' shops. At a fountain ahead of him two old hags were beating linen. As he passed them they squatted back on their haunches, stared, and then their 'A-hak-kak-kak!' with the slap, slap, of the stone on the linen sounded after him.

He reached the top of the hill; he turned a corner and the town was hidden. Down he looked into a deep valley with a dried-up river bed at the bottom. This side and that was covered with small dilapidated houses that had broken stone verandas where the fruit lay drying, tomato lanes in the garden and from the gates to the doors a trellis of vines. The late sunlight, deep, golden, lay in the cup of the valley; there was a smell of charcoal in the air. In the gardens the men were cutting grapes. He watched a man standing in the greenish shade, raising up, holding a black cluster in one hand, taking the knife from his belt, cutting, laying the bunch in a flat boat-shaped basket. The man worked leisurely, silently, taking hundreds of years over the job. On the hedges on the other side of the road there were grapes small as berries, growing wild, growing among the stones. He leaned against a wall, filled his pipe, put a match to it . . .

Leaned across a gate, turned up the collar of his mackintosh. It was going to rain. It didn't matter, he was prepared for it. You didn't expect anything else in November. He looked over the bare field. From the corner by the gate there came the smell of swedes, a great stack of them, wet, rank coloured. Two men passed walking towards the straggling village. 'Good day!' 'Good day!' By Jove! He had to hurry if he was going to catch that train home. Over the gate, across a field, over the stile, into the lane, swinging along in the drifting rain and dusk . . . Just home in time for a bath and a change before supper. . . . In the drawing-room; Jinnie is sitting pretty nearly in the fire. 'Oh, Robert, I didn't hear you come in. Did you have a good time? How nice you smell! A present?' 'Some bits of blackberry I picked for you. Pretty colour.' 'Oh, lovely, Robert! Dennis and Beaty are coming to supper.' Supper – cold beef, potatoes in their jackets, claret, household bread. They are gay – everybody's laughing. 'Oh, we all know Robert,' says Dennis, breathing on his eyeglasses and polishing them. 'By the way, Dennis, I picked up a very jolly little edition of . . .'

A clock struck. He wheeled sharply. What time was it. Five? A quarter past? Back, back the way he came. As he passed through the gates he saw her on the look-out. She got up, waved and slowly she came to meet him, dragging the heavy cape. In her hand she carried a spray of heliotrope.

'You're late,' she cried gaily. 'You're three minutes late. Here's your watch, it's been very good while you were away. Did you have a nice time? Was it lovely? Tell me. Where did you go?'

'I say – put this *on*,' he said, taking the cape from her.

'Yes, I will. Yes, it's getting chilly. Shall we go up to our room?'

When they reached the lift she was coughing. He frowned.

'It's nothing. I haven't been out too late. Don't be cross.'

She sat down on one of the red plush chairs while he rang and rang, and then, getting no answer, kept his finger on the bell.

'Oh, Robert, do you think you ought to?'

'Ought to what?'

The door of the *salon* opened. 'What is that? Who is making that noise?' sounded from within. Klaymongso began to yelp. 'Caw! Caw! Caw!' came from the General. A Topknot darted out with one hand to her ear, opened the staff door, 'Mr Queet! Mr Queet!' she bawled. That brought the manager up at a run.

'Is that you ringing the bell, Mr Salesby? Do you want the lift? Very good, sir. I'll take you up myself. Antonio wouldn't have been a minute, he was just taking off his apron – ' And having ushered them in, the oily manager went to the door of the *salon*. 'Very sorry you should have been troubled, ladies and gentlemen.' Salesby stood in the cage, sucking in his cheeks, staring at the ceiling and turning the ring, turning the signet ring on his little finger. . . .

Arrived in their room he went swiftly to the washstand, shook the bottle, poured her out a dose and brought it across.

'Sit down. Drink it. And don't talk.' And he stood over her while she obeyed. Then he took the glass, rinsed it and put it back in its case. 'Would you like a cushion?'

'No, I'm quite all right. Come over here. Sit down by me just a minute, will you, Robert? Ah, that's very nice.' She turned and thrust the piece of heliotrope in the lapel of his coat. 'That,' she said, 'is most becoming.' And then she leaned her head against his shoulder and he put his arm round her.

'Robert –' her voice like a sigh – like a breath.

'Yes – '

They sat there for a long while. The sky flamed, paled; the two white beds were like two ships. . . . At last he heard the servant girl running along the corridor with the hot-water cans, and gently he released her and turned on the light.

'Oh, what time is it? Oh, what a heavenly evening. Oh, Robert, I was thinking while you were away this afternoon . . .'

They were the last couple to enter the dining-room. The Countess was there with her lorgnette and her fan, the General was there with his special chair and the air cushion and the small rug over his knees. The American Woman was there showing Klaymongso a copy of the *Saturday Evening Post*. . . . 'We're having a feast of reason and a flow of soul.' The Two Topknots were there feeling over the peaches and the pears in their dish of fruit and putting aside all they considered unripe or overripe to show to the manager, and the Honeymoon Couple leaned across the table, whispering, trying not to burst out laughing.

Mr Queet, in everyday clothes and white canvas shoes, served the soup, and Antonio, in full evening dress, handed it round.

'No,' said the American Woman, 'take it away, Antonio. We can't eat soup. We can't eat anything mushy, can we, Klaymongso?'

'Take them back and fill them to the rim!' said the Topknots, and they turned and watched while Antonio delivered the message.

'What is it? Rice? Is it cooked?' The Countess peered through her lorgnette. 'Mr Queet, the General can have some of this soup if it is cooked.'

'Very good, Countess.'

The Honeymoon Couple had their fish instead.

'Give me that one. That's the one I caught. No, it's not. Yes, it is. No, it's not. Well it's looking at me with its eye, so it must be. Tee! Hee! Hee!' Their feet were locked together under the table.

'Robert, you're not eating again. Is anything the matter?'

'No. Off food, that's all.'

'Oh, what a bother. There are eggs and spinach coming. You don't like spinach, do you. I must tell them in future . . .'

An egg and mashed potatoes for the General.

'Mr Queet! Mr Queet!'

'Yes, Countess.'

'The General's egg's too hard again.'

'Caw! Caw! Caw!'

'Very sorry, Countess. Shall I have you another cooked, General?'

. . . They are the first to leave the dining-room. She rises, gathering her shawl and he stands aside, waiting for her to pass, turning the ring, turning the signet ring on his little finger. In the hall Mr Queet hovers. 'I thought you might not want to wait for the lift. Antonio's just serving the finger bowls. And I'm sorry the bell won't ring, it's out of order. I can't think what's happened.'

'Oh, I do hope . . .' from her.

'Get in,' says he.

Mr Queet steps after them and slams the door . . .

'. . . Robert, do you mind if I go to bed very soon? Won't you go down to the *salon* or out into the garden? Or perhaps you might smoke a cigar on the balcony. It's lovely out there. And I like cigar smoke. I always did. But if you'd rather . . .'

'No, I'll sit here.'

He takes a chair and sits on the balcony. He hears her moving about in the room, lightly, lightly, moving and rustling. Then she comes over to him. 'Good night, Robert.'

'Good night.' He takes her hand and kisses the palm. 'Don't catch cold.'

The sky is the colour of jade. There are a great many stars; an enormous white moon hangs over the garden. Far away lightning flutters – flutters like a wing – flutters like a broken bird that tries to fly and sinks again and again struggles.

The lights from the *salon* shine across the garden path and there is the sound of a piano. And once the American Woman, opening the French window to let Klaymongso into the garden, cries: 'Have you seen this moon?' But nobody answers.

He gets very cold sitting there, staring at the balcony rail. Finally he comes inside. The moon – the room is painted white with moonlight. The light trembles in the mirrors; the two beds seem to float. She is asleep. He sees her through the nets, half sitting, banked up with pillows, her white hands crossed on the sheet. Her white cheeks, her fair hair pressed against the pillow, are silvered over. He undresses quickly, stealthily and gets into bed. Lying there, his hands clasped behind his head.

. . . In his study. Late summer. The virginia creeper just on the turn. . . .

'Well, my dear chap, that's the whole story. That's the long and the short of it. If she can't cut away for the next two years and give a decent climate a chance she don't stand a dog's – h'm – show. Better be frank about these things.' 'Oh, certainly. . . .' 'And hang it all, old man, what's to prevent you going with her? It isn't as though you've got a regular job like us wage earners. You can do what you do wherever you are – ' 'Two years.' 'Yes, I should give it two years. You'll have no trouble about letting this house, you know. As a matter of fact . . .'

. . . He is with her. 'Robert, the awful thing is – I suppose it's my illness – I simply feel I could not go alone. You see – you're everything. You're bread and wine, Robert, bread and wine. Oh, my darling – what am I saying? Of course I could, of course I won't take you away . . .'

He hears her stirring. Does she want something?

'Boogles?'

Good Lord! She is talking in her sleep. They haven't used that name for years.

'Boogles. Are you awake?'

'Yes, do you want anything?'

'Oh, I'm going to be a bother. I'm so sorry. Do you mind? There's a wretched mosquito inside my net – I can hear him singing. Would you catch him? I don't want to move because of my heart.'

'No, don't move. Stay where you are.' He switches on the light, lifts the net. 'Where is the little beggar? Have you spotted him?'

'Yes, there, over by the corner. Oh, I do feel such a fiend to have dragged you out of bed. Do you mind dreadfully?'

'No, of course not.' For a moment he hovers in his blue and white pyjamas. Then, 'got him,' he said.

'Oh, good. Was he a juicy one?'

'Beastly.' He went over to the washstand and dipped his fingers in water. 'Are you all right now? Shall I switch off the light?'

'Yes, please. No. Boogles! Come back here a moment. Sit down by me. Give me your hand.' She turns his signet ring. 'Why weren't you asleep? Boogles, listen. Come closer. I sometimes wonder – do you mind awfully being out here with me?'

He bends down. He kisses her. He tucks her in, he smooths the pillow.

'Rot!' he whispers.

Critical approaches through contexts

Any text is engaged in a number of contexts. These can be:

intertextual or literary contexts such as genre, literary conventions, and relationship to other texts by the same writer or other contemporary writers;

historical contexts relating to the political, social and economic conditions at the time of the text's production;

biographical contexts, relating to the author's life;

cultural contexts, referring to the beliefs and values of a society and its other cultural products, such as film or art.

Likewise, any *reader* is engaged in a number of contexts, which may well be very different from those of the writing of the text. If we take three main headings for contexts here, biographical, historical and literary we can consider in more detail how they might shape the meanings we find in the story.

Biographical

Katherine Mansfield 1888–1923

It is important to be careful in how you use biographical information. Students often turn to it with relief as if it must be the best source of information about the meaning of a text. As we have seen earlier in this book, many critics argue that the reader is as important as the writer in making the meaning of a text. The idea that the writer must be the ultimate authority, along with the use of the word 'author', has been criticised and the author was famously declared 'dead'. Giving factual information about an author is usually easy compared to analysing the text, so you should not rely on this as a substantial part of an essay. You must show that anything you say about a writer's life is precisely relevant to the text under discussion. In the case of Mansfield's text, consider whether the following information would be useful.

The story is set in an expatriate community. Mansfield grew up in colonial New Zealand. She moved to Europe at the age of 18 but continued to feel, and be regarded as, an 'outsider'. She did, however, become closely involved in the literary circles of London, knowing writers such as D.H. Lawrence and Virginia Woolf who were engaged in debates about writing 'modern fiction'. Mansfield suffered from tuberculosis and stayed in hotels in warm parts of Europe for her health. When she wrote this particular story she wanted her husband, John Middleton Murray, to come and stay with her, but he remained in England. She died at the age of 34. It is interesting that critics have interpreted the husband in the story as a hostile portrait of Mansfield's own husband, but much later he commented that he thought Robert was in fact an admirable figure!

Historical and cultural

In 1919 the recently ended 1914–1918 war, in which millions of men died fighting in Europe, was very significant. Mansfield's brother was a volunteer who died in 1915. The traumatic experiences of the First World War were profound and led to a sense of disillusionment and loss of faith. The sense of sickness and instability is very strong in *The Man Without a Temperament* and perhaps reflects this sense of decay and corruption. At the same time there are other shifts in society, some due in part to the war, others developing from social and political movements of previous decades. Attitudes to the Empire, so strong at the turn of the century, have changed, as have social class relations. The colonial world which the residents try to maintain in the story is shown to be collapsing and temporary. The description of the Hotel Hall depicts a collision of cultures: the Notice of Services at the English Church, the umbrellas and the 'Presentation' clock are set alongside the palms which are described as 'ancient beggars', implying the relationship of the colonised to the colonisers. It is a world askew, defunct and neglected: the letters are unclaimed and the clock strikes the hours at the half hours. There is a sense of transience and impermanence as the luggage is 'piled-up' in the corridor. The residents are preserved in this decadent artificial world while the 'natural' world threatens its thresholds: 'a great creeping thing ... hungrily watching her'.

The campaign for women's right to vote was rewarded after the war and the changes in attitudes towards women and the possibilities for different relationships between the sexes were also a debate amongst the social circles in which Mansfield moved. In the story two marriages are contrasted – the barren marriage of dependency and obligation and the passionate sexuality of the honeymoon couple. The 'other' world outside is also charged up with sensuality and sexual descriptions: 'every leaf, every flower in the garden lay open, motionless, as if exhausted, and a sweet, rich, rank smell filled the quivering air'.

Social and economic hierarchies are also expressed through the landscape as Robert moves away from Pension Villa Excelsior (the name itself associates this world with Christianity, commerce and elitism) past the residences of the rich, followed by the tradesmen who service them and then to the world of the peasants. In the hotel, the servants come from diverse cultures, but unlike the cosy cohesive view of servant/master relationship longingly conjured up in Robert's daydreams, they seem subversive, not answering the lift bell for example. The story is characterised throughout by a sense of impending collapse, not only of the sick woman, but the unstable societies represented in the story.

Literary contexts

Literary critics and historians often give labels such as 'modernism' to eras that seem characterised by particular developments, ideas or reactions against the past. Whole decades can be summed up in such terms (for example 'Romanticism') but it is important to remember that the boundaries, dates and characteristics are defined in retrospect and this in itself imposes a shape and coherence on that period and its texts, which the participants at the time might not have felt at all. However, the writers we now call 'modernist' were conscious of changing the literary landscape. Virginia Woolf even proposed a 'starting date' for it: '. . . in or about December 1910 human character changed'! In fact many critics trace the developments back into the last part of the nineteenth century, but the height of modernism is regarded as 1910 to 1930 when novelists like Joyce, Woolf and Lawrence were writing and poets like T.S. Eliot were also changing the expectations of poetry. Literary movements are not the spontaneous work of writers but are inextricably tied into their historical moment. There was a reaction against the moral certainties and authorities of the Victorian era, particularly as represented in the realist novel with its authorial control and confident, closed narratives (see Chapter 4). Writers now argued that 'life' could not be contained or expressed by neat plots and carefully judged characters and the moralising omniscient narrator seemed inappropriate. Sigmund Freud's ideas about psychoanalysis, which were being published from the 1890s onwards, depicted the mind as only partially knowable and emphasised the significance of the subconscious revealed, for example, through dreams. The writing technique developed by some modernist writers to reflect the messy, disorganised experience of subjectivity or thought processes is sometimes called an 'interior monologue' or 'stream of consciousness'. Modernist writing is often interested in symbolism and patterns of imagery and uses poetic techniques. This can make the work quite challenging for the reader because there is no particular guide and the writing can be shifting and fragmentary, more concerned with the failure of communication than with establishing it. The writers were very self-conscious and drew attention to the processes of art, rather than maintaining the idea of writing as a reflection of the world.

The short story was a very suitable form to work in, because, unlike the realist novel with its emphasis on plot – a series of connected events and causal relationships, it could focus on the moment in an otherwise disordered subject. This is sometimes called an 'epiphany' where there is a brief sense of significance or revelation. Mansfield concentrated on the short story. The influence of modernism helps explain the disjointed, self-conscious and poetic nature of this short story. The lack of authority in the narrative explains the disorientation the reader experiences in the opening paragraphs. The writing slips from authorial voice to direct speech to free indirect speech in ways that can be confusing: 'Sometimes she even pointed at it, crying: 'Isn't that the most terrible thing you've seen! Isn't that ghoulish!' It was on the other side of the veranda, after all . . . and besides it couldn't touch her, could it Klaymongso?' The shifts in scene that occur in the story as we enter Robert's daydreams are also striking and unconventional. Perhaps the writing was also influenced by the developments in cinema at the time where such juxtapositions of scenes were being employed. The story deals with failure of communication (in the marriage) but is more broadly concerned with the limited capacities of expression and connection in this society.

Think again about the story in the light of what you have read.

What do you think is meant by the final word spoken in the story, 'Rot'?

Modern fiction in 1919

In 1919 Virginia Woolf published an influential essay, entitled *Modern Fiction* in which she criticised the conventions of realism. She was particularly hostile to the conventions of what she calls the 'materialists'; Edwardian writers who incorporated highly detailed settings and appearances in their fiction. The following is an extract from it:

Nevertheless, we go on perseveringly conscientiously, constructing our two and thirty chapters after a design which more and more ceases to resemble the vision in our minds. So much of the enormous labour of proving the solidity, the likeness to life, of the story is not merely labour thrown away but labour misplaced to the extent of obscuring and blotting out the light of the conception. The writer seems constrained, not by his own free will but by some powerful and unscrupulous tyrant who has him in thrall, to provide a plot, to provide comedy, tragedy, love, interest, and an air of probability embalming the whole so impeccably that if all his figures were to come to life they would find themselves dressed down to the last button of their coats in the fashion of the hour. The tyrant is obeyed; the novel is done to a turn. But sometimes, more and more often as time goes by, we suspect a momentary doubt, a spasm of rebellion, as the pages fill themselves in the customary way. Is life like this? Must novels be like this?

Look within and life, it seems, is very far from being 'like this'. Examine for a moment an ordinary mind on an ordinary day. The mind receives a myriad impressions – trivial, fantastic, evanescent, or engraved with the sharpness of steel. From all sides they come, an incessant show of innumerable atoms; and as they fall, as they shape themselves into the life of a Monday or a Tuesday, the accent falls differently from old; the moment of importance came not here but there. . . . Life is not a series of gig lamps* symmetrically arranged; life is a luminous halo, a semi-transparent envelope surrounding us from the beginnings of consciousness to the end. Is it not the task of the novelist to convey this varying, this unknown and uncircumscribed spirit, whatever aberration or complexity it may display, with as little mixture of the alien and external as possible? We are not pleading merely for courage and sincerity; we are suggesting that the proper stuff of fiction is a little other than custom would have us believe it.

* gig lamps – the lamps hung on either side of a gig, a light carriage or an old fashioned word for spectacles.

ACTIVITY 33

In your own words sum up the contrast between the two types of writing that Woolf describes here. Then discuss in pairs whether or not her ideas apply to your reading of the short story that Mansfield was writing around the same time.

You should now be in a position to try out some short pieces of writing to compare the styles Woolf is writing about in this essay.

ACTIVITY 34

First, have a go at a realist piece, based on the passage from Jane Eyre at the beginning of this chapter. Spend some time recalling an incident from your childhood in which you were angry with a relative or they were angry with you. Jot down as many details as you can about where and when it took place, the appearance of people, rooms and objects. You should write using the all-knowing narrator, the past tense and some dialogue. You can, of course, 'fictionalise' the incident, particularly as you may not be able to recall what was said or descriptive detail.

For your second piece, sit with a pen and paper in a place where there is some activity or plenty to see. Look around you and concentrate on your sense impressions as well as the ideas passing through your mind. When you start to write you should aim to continue for ten minutes. Write in the present tense and try to convey all the experience of those minutes.

Look at your pieces of writing. You might like to share them with someone else in your group. Which do you feel worked best and why?

In this chapter you have considered how some of the writers of the early twentieth century reacted to the classic realism of the nineteenth century. You have focused on the importance of developing an understanding of the contexts of writing, which is one of the assessment objectives at AS level; evaluating the significance of such contexts is assessed at A2 level.

7 From the Twentieth to the Twenty-first Century: Postmodernism

In this chapter you will learn about some of the developments in prose fiction over the second half of the twentieth century. You will work closely on a complete short story and consider the writer's commentary on her story.

The death of the novel?

Since the experiments of **modernism**, which we considered in the last chapter, there have been almost continual announcements of the 'death' of the novel. Writers, critics and newspaper columnists have claimed that fiction writing has become moribund, that novelists are no longer able to write in significant ways about important subjects. Quite often this seems to mean the death of the kind of novel that nineteenth century writers produced and that, it is fair to say, the modernists had a go at killing off. This makes good stories for newspapers that like to see a bit of fighting and bloodshed in the rather un-newsworthy and non-polemical world of fiction publication. However, it is the case that since the early decades of the twentieth century, there has been continuing experimentation with fiction and a quest for novels to express their age that looks back rather romantically at the confidence with which, it is claimed, nineteenth century writers were able to express theirs. While the modernist writers were often seen as having a gloomy response to this loss of faith and certainty, it is argued that what are often called postmodernist texts choose instead to revel in it. Other critics do not like the label of **postmodernism** because they see the literary landscape as a continuation from modernism and not sufficiently different to be 'post', which means after or following. There were a lot of 'post' terms around in the late twentieth century, such as postcolonial or postfeminism and they can be used to suggest a break with the past, as if colonialism or feminist were all done with now: all labels tend to package things up. Equally, they can draw our attention to important concepts. The term postcolonial, for example, makes visible and relevant the practice of colonialism – the occupation and exploitation of a nation by another – which is perhaps not as dead and buried as we'd like it to be.

So what is postmodernism?

Postmodernism is a rather wide and loose term, which covers ways of thinking, critical ideas in literary theory and ways of writing texts. It can be used even more generally in terms like 'the postmodern condition' to describe the economic and cultural climate of late twentieth century Western society with the particular brands of technologies, commercialism and consumer culture associated with this. If the term itself seems rather all-inclusive and hard to pin down, then that might also be said of the texts it produces. Postmodernism does not accept the distinctions between 'high' culture and 'low' culture and can be interested in the everyday and popular. The texts are often described as 'playful' in the ways that they mix genres and conventions so that they constantly play with or parody other types of texts, such as historical texts, in order to draw attention to the ways all texts are constructed rather than 'true'. History is seen, for example, as just another story, rather than a privileged, authoritative story that must be believed. Big philosophical ideas, such as Christianity or Marxism, that seem to explain the world, are also seen as stories or 'grand narratives' that can no longer be considered as all-important.

In fiction writing, the conventions of realism are often played with. One genre that has received a lot of interest recently has been 'magic realism', which brings fantastic elements into realistic settings, so that a character might grow wings for example, or sit in a deckchair and be slowly absorbed into the ground. Many South American writers have produced magic realist books, having lived through political systems where incredible events, such as people suddenly disappearing without trace, or history being 'rewritten' by political authorities, have been 'realities'.

Revising fairy tales

Other writers have revisited other traditional genres, such as myths or fairy tales and recast them in blends of the fantastic and realistic. This has often been associated with feminist writers who have used traditionally patriarchal (male-dominated) stories to revise gender relations.

The following extract is from the beginning of a short story called *The Bloody Chamber*, written by Angela Carter. It is based on the traditional tale of Bluebeard, the rich man who marries a young girl from a poor family and takes her to his castle. When he leaves his new wife alone in the castle, he gives her a set of keys but instructs her never to open the door of one room. Overcome by curiosity she enters the room to find the murdered bodies of his previous wives. The message of the tale as originally told in the 1697 collection by Perrault, seems to warn women about the dangers of disobedience and curiosity.

ACTIVITY 35

Read the extract from Angela Carter's story carefully, discussing in pairs its language and style and the effect it produces upon the reader. You should include the following questions in your discussion:

- What kinds of stories does the writing remind you of?
- What kind of world does the story seem to be set in?
- What ideas are offered about men and women?

I remember how, that night, I lay awake in the wagon-lit in a tender, delicious ecstasy of excitement, my burning cheek pressed against the impeccable linen of the pillow and the pounding of my heart mimicking that of the great pistons ceaselessly thrusting the train that bore me through the night, away from Paris, away from girlhood, away from the white, enclosed quietude of my mother's apartment, into the unguessable country of marriage.

And I remember I tenderly imagined how, at this very moment, my mother would be moving slowly about the narrow bedroom I had left behind for ever, folding up and putting away all my little relics, the tumbled garments I would not need any more, the scores for which there had been no room in my trunks, the concert programmes I'd abandoned; she would linger over this torn ribbon and that faded photograph with all the half-joyous, half-sorrowful emotions of a woman on her daughter's wedding day. And, in the midst of my bridal triumph, I felt a pang of loss as if, when he put the gold band on my finger, I had, in some way, ceased to be her child in becoming his wife. . . .

Now and then a starburst of lights spattered the drawn blinds as if the railway company had lit up all the stations through which we passed in celebration of the bride. My satin nightdress had just been shaken from its wrappings; it had slipped over my young girl's pointed breasts and shoulders, supple as a garment of heavy water, and now teasingly caressed me, egregious, insinuating, nudging between my thighs as I shifted restlessly in my narrow berth. His kiss, his kiss with tongue and teeth in it and a rasp of beard, had hinted to me, though with the same exquisite tact as this nightdress he'd given me, of the wedding night, which would be voluptuously deferred until we lay in his great ancestral bed in the sea-girt, pinnacled domain that lay, still, beyond the grasp of my imagination . . . that magic place, the fairy castle whose walls were made of foam, that legendary habitation in which he had been born. To which, one day, I might bear an heir. Our destination, my destiny.

COMMENTARY The opening paragraph consists of one long sentence, creating a sense of the urgency of the transport the narrator is engaged in – both a literal and a metaphorical journey, passing from one 'place' to another. She is moving from child to adult, from poverty to wealth; from the centre of the city to the land's edge; from the matriarchal world of the mother to the patriarchal world of men. There is a very powerful sense of a significant transition in the opening paragraphs. It reminds the reader of several different texts or discourses, such as the breathless prose of romance: 'delicious ecstasy of excitement'; the detail of social realist novels; the teasing of pornographic texts with the vulnerable girl and predatory beast; and of course the fairy tale. The text is playing with a number of genres and later on brings in many references to other texts and other cultural products such as music, film and art. The figure of Bluebeard enjoys and possesses both 'high' art and pornographic art: he represents both the 'height' and the 'decadence' of Western civilisation and the story seems to be set in a 'fin-de-siecle' France with one foot in the old, another in the new century. It has many of the characteristics of the **Gothic**, which we looked at in Chapter 5, in its evocation of an ancient code of oppression. The ancestral nature of this tyranny is reinforced here by the great bed and the 'legendary habitation in which he had been born'. The woman's place in this is to provide an heir to carry on the legacy of this social system. In fact, in the original story it is the father that the girl is separated from and her move to adult sexuality is confirmed by the transfer from father to husband and she is rescued by her brothers as Bluebeard is about to kill her. In Carter's updated story, the alternative world she moves from is a maternal one and it is the mother whose instincts send her rushing off to kill Bluebeard before he can murder her daughter.

ACTIVITY 36

The next text for you to read is a complete short story by an American writer, Joyce Carol Oates, which is also based on the Bluebeard story. It was first published in 1988. Try to get hold of a copy of Perrault's original tale and a complete text of Angela Carter's *The Bloody Chamber* and compare the different treatments of this story.

Blue-Bearded Lover

I.
When we walked together he held my hand unnaturally high, at the level of his chest, as no man had done before. In this way he made his claim.

When we stood at night beneath the great winking sky he instructed me gently in its deceit. The stars you see above you, he said, have vanished thousands of millions of years ago; it is precisely the stars you cannot see that exist, and exert their influence upon you.

When we lay together in the tall cold grasses the grasses curled lightly over us as if to hide us.

II.
A man's passion is his triumph, I have learned. And to be the receptacle of a man's passion is a woman's triumph.

III.
He made me his bride and brought me to his great house which smelled of time and death. Passageways and doors and high-ceilinged rooms and tall windows opening out onto nothing. Have you ever loved another man as you now love me? my blue-bearded lover asked. Do you give your life to me?

What is a woman's life that cannot be thrown away!

He told me of the doors I may unlock and the rooms I may enter freely. He told me of the seventh door, the forbidden door, which I may not unlock: for behind it lies a forbidden room which I may not enter. Why may I not enter it? I asked, for I saw that he expected it of me, and he said, kissing my brow, Because I have forbidden it.

And he entrusted me with the key to the door, for he was going away on a long journey.

IV.
Here it is: a small golden key, weighing no more than a feather in the palm of my hand.

It is faintly stained as if with blood. It glistens when I hold it to the light.

Did I not know that my lover's previous brides had been brought to this house to die? – that they had failed him, one by one, and had deserved their fate?

I have slipped the golden key into my bosom, to wear against my heart, as a token of my lover's trust in me.

V.
When my blue-bearded lover returned from his long journey he was gratified to see that the door to the forbidden room remained locked; and when he examined the key, still warm from my bosom, he saw that the stain was an old, old stain, and not of my doing.

And he declared with great passion that I was now truly his wife; and that he loved me above all women.

VI.
Through the opened windows the invisible stars exert their power.

But if it is a power that is known, are the stars invisible?

When I sleep in our sumptuous bed I sleep deeply, and dream dreams that I cannot remember afterward, of extraordinary beauty, I think, and magic, and wonder. Sometimes in the morning my husband will recall them for me, for their marvels are such they invade even his dreams. How is it that you of all persons can dream such dreams, he says, – such curious works of art!

And he kisses me, and seems to forgive me.

And I will be bearing his child soon. The first of his many children.

Blue-Bearded Lover is written in a very different style from Angela Carter's story: it is very bare and minimal in contrast to the lush, rich descriptive prose of *The Bloody Chamber*. It is more like a prose poem, divided into stanzas (you might like to compare this use of form with the story by Jayne Anne Phillips in Chapter 3). Oates also changes the original story, but unlike Carter who rescues her narrator from Bluebeard's clutches, this speaker already knows the ghastly contents of the locked room and so 'passes' the test. Both stories are exploring the nature of power in relationships, but Angela Carter's story locates ideas about power in a historical and cultural context. Society is not visible in Oates' story; she uses the metaphor of the stars to raise questions about power. You may find Oates's story more unsettling, even disturbing in the controlled voice with which the narrator accepts the terms of her situation. Who do you feel has power by the end of this short story?

Examining postmodernist writing

As we have seen in earlier chapters, the study of English literature, specifically prose fiction, has been very closely tied up with realism. There were, of course, playful texts written in the eighteenth and nineteenth centuries as well, the most famous being Laurence Sterne's *Tristram Shandy*. This novel was dismissed as too silly and trivial to be included in Leavis's Great Tradition (see Chapter 2) as the realist novel was established as the most important to study. The traditional tools of analysis at A level, characters, plot, themes and language, have developed to suit that particular genre of prose very well. When we examine texts, like the modernist text in the previous chapter, these tools are still useful because we can see how the modernist writer disrupts and reconfigures them. Modernism set itself against realism so the conventions are thrown into the air, but the student can engage in debate with them in a broadly familiar way. Postmodernist writers also reject the conventions of realism such as character and plot and the coherence or clear meanings of such novels. It can be challenging to think how we can analyse a text which does not offer the reader carefully constructed fictional characters and relationships within an organised plot in an identifiable genre and style.

The complete short story you are about to work on was written by Alison MacLeod and revised for this book. Alison MacLeod was brought up in Canada and now teaches English and Creative Writing at University College, Chichester. She has had many short stories published. Her novel *The Changeling* was published in 1996 and she is currently completing her second novel, *Mirabilis*. This story draws on the famous figure of Princess Diana, who died in a car crash in a tunnel in Paris in 1997. If you can recall this event, or images of Diana, then spend a few minutes talking about these in a small group. Then carefully read through the story twice.

Dreaming Diana: Twelve Frames

1

In 1981, I had the Lady Di. I went to Wendy's Hair Salon on the Bedford Highway and asked for the Lady Di because I didn't know the name of any other haircut, except for the Farrah Fawcett, and I didn't have the nerve to ask for those feathery wings that were emblematic of Farrah's pin-up glory. I thought I could manage the Lady Di. She worried about her nose. She bit her nails. I could see she did every time I reached for a cookie from the commemorative cake tin with the engagement picture on it.

Wendy did my hair herself, and didn't laugh when I asked for the Lady Di, but even Wendy, sucking hard on her cigarette, couldn't work that magic. I emerged from the salon onto the highway looking like a dishevelled pageboy.

That same summer, I fell in love with Stephen Murray. He was tall. He had a shy wit. And he spelled his name with a 'ph' instead of a 'v'. In my 16-year old terms, it made him complicated.

It was the last dance of the school year. Midsummer's night. The dance was not in the high school gym, but at the Harbour Boat Club. Gone was the smell of rubber crash mats and adolescent sweat. Gone, the generalised threat of gym ropes and foul lines. Instead we stepped onto a sunken dance floor with parquet tiles. We became wall flowers against festoons of crepe-paper streamers and bright Chinese lanterns. Outside, on the long, low verandah, boys were threatening to let the girls in their arms drop into the tide below while, above us all, the Northern Lights shook the night sky.

I can't remember any music. I only remember that as Stephen Murray and I started to dance, he turned me on my heels and my new summer skirt took life, floating wide as a water lily on the air.

We walked through the night together. We tried to remember what caused the Northern Lights and couldn't. He smiled. We dropped stones into the waves below. He took my hand in his.

So when he crossed the threshold, moments before the last waltz, with a tall, thoroughbred of a girl called Diana – a girl no one had ever seen, a girl from out of town – the magic of the night forked like lightning. I envied her her name, but even more than that, I envied her her hair. She had a perfect Lady Di, a cloud of gold dipping over one eye.

Like everyone that summer, I watched the Royal Wedding and cried.

2

Almost two years later, I couldn't explain to myself why I was waiting to see Diana. The lobby of the Hotel Nova Scotian was empty. We had arrived with two-and-a-half hours to spare. 'Phew!' I said to my sister. 'We made it.'

A British photographer was asleep on his feet against a pillar. Ellen wanted to go home. I rooted in my bag and pulled out the camera our parents had given me for graduation that year. Ellen rolled her eyes. 'Tell me you're not going to take pictures.' I played with the insta-matic shutter and said nothing. But in my mind's eye, I could already see Diana's foot stepping onto the red carpet the two bellboys were unfurling before us. She would be moving. Smiling. Extending her hand. Perhaps she would say a few words in passing. All in three dimensions.

We got through the bag of Licorice All Sorts Ellen had in her schoolbag. We found two pens and played tic-tac-toe on her restless legs. For a long time, we watched the British photographer not wake up, and, all the while, we held our ground against the gathering horde. The lobby was hot now, airless. The oddly fitting top I had made in Home-Ec that year was sticking to my armpits, and my Kodak Disc camera was sweating like old money in my hands.

Yet when the moment was at last upon us, I hesitated. Trudeau walked through the door in his white dinner jacket. She was just moments behind. Was it better to watch her 'live' – perhaps shake her hand – or get a picture? A picture of a picture coming to life.

She was wearing a cream-coloured ballgown and a tiara. Her hair was longer than I'd seen in any of the photos, and she was very slim. She would have looked fragile if it weren't for the strength of that wide, toothpaste smile.

She was shaking hands, smiling, saying hello, asking the occasional question. I remember the strangeness of hearing her voice as I watched her through my camera's red viewfinder. She stopped and spoke to the hotel receptionist next to Ellen. For a moment, I felt self-conscious as I pointed the camera at her. Rude. Then I took the picture.

Later, everyone marvelled that I'd been so close, that I'd managed to get such a good picture. 'She looks beautiful,' they said. 'She's even prettier in real life,' I heard myself say. They waited for a spree of adjectives, for my eyewitness account, for the flush of a young woman's excitement, but I went dumb. I knew I couldn't describe the light of her. It wasn't flashbulbs. Or an aura. Or a halo. Or the glamour of a blonde. Or the radiance of a new bride. Or the glow of a pregnant woman. It wasn't any of those things.

Afterwards, I stuck the snap in a new album. I took care to avoid ripples of air as I pressed it under the transparent sheet. But I knew it wasn't what I'd wanted.

You can't get a picture of a picture coming to life. It's just another picture.

3

They say, you wouldn't have known to look at her; that her face was unchanged except for the bruise under one eye.

At the private mortuary in Fulham, the post-mortem was conducted in the middle of the night. Her body was guarded throughout by officers from Special Branch. An official photographer was brought in to document the minutiae of the proceedings. Such intimacies.

He was escorted to the toilet, twice. He was searched upon entering the premises, and again when leaving. For what? A stashed film?

Too obvious.

They frisked him for a bit of hair. For a sample of body fluid. For a sacred scraping of DNA. They couldn't risk a tabloid relic. A black market dream. A national security crisis.

4

'Is she real dead or pretend dead?' a small girl asked her mother outside St. James' Palace, where her body rested.

Princesses on biers open their eyes again.

5

Once upon a time, long before our time or our mothers' time, Sleeping Beauty awoke not merely to a kiss, but to the unmistakable sight of her second trimester.

In Paris in late July, I had found myself staring at front-page tabloid snaps of Diana, side on. She was walking barefoot on a sandy beach, wearing a one-piece swimsuit – an animal print. Her head was down. She was refusing to look the way of the off-shore boats. Her arms were folded at her front.

Perhaps her posture was, at that moment, poor. Perhaps she had a genuine tummy. Or bloating that day. Then again, perhaps there are things that only a coroner will ever know.

'DIANA ENCEINTE?'* the tabloids speculated that day in bold face.

She was a vessel to fill.

6

'In my dream she'd been cremated,' said Anna Sharland of Manchester. 'And I had the urn, you know the safekeeping of the ashes, and the whole country knew. But my daughter Suzanna spilled them all over the floor. I scooped them back into the urn as well as I could – I had to fool people – but I knew there were bits of stair-carpet in there. It was awful.'

7

They killed her because she was dabbling in politics. Because she was turning to the Left. Because she had loose lips. Because she was about to marry an Arab. Because she was going to convert to Islam, like her friend Jemima Khan. Because she was carrying an illegitimate, half-Arab baby. Because Charles could never otherwise have Camilla. Because she was part of a psychic task-force and knew what They were up to.

Perhaps she wasn't the only one. Not long before her death, BBC journalists had practised in private a 'sudden and violent death scenario' – intended to cover travel accident, assassination or suicide – involving Princess Diana.

On the BBC, she was Our Lady of Sorrows. On ITV, Diana the Martyred. On Sky, appropriately, Diana the Goddess. Spectacularly sacrificed.

8

Shehnaz Shafi, 39, a Pakistani who had had his photo taken with the Princess the previous May in his village near Lahore, poisoned himself after hearing of her death. In Hong Kong, a young man jumped out of the 33rd floor of a tower block. A pile of cuttings about her death was found nearby.

9

The day before the funeral, I took a morning train to London. On arrival, I stopped at Victoria and selected an expensive bunch of miniature pink roses, though I had planned restraint. I reminded myself I'd never known the woman.

My excuse was curiosity. It was a phenomenon like no other, I had told my husband. Maybe it was History, I'd mumbled, embarrassed. At the very least, it was surreal. Later, on the phone to my parents in Nova Scotia, I would describe for them my position on the Royal Mile when the Union Flag was finally lowered over Buckingham Palace. I would conjure the smell of those seas of decaying blooms. I would tell my mother that the Queen and the Duke had waved and smiled as they were driven into St. James' Palace to see her body. And I would tell them about the queue that never ended as people came from all over the country to sign the books of condolence.

I didn't tell them I tried, too late, to join the queue. I was too shamefaced to say that I'd been drawn to London by rumours of visions in the Palace where her body was resting; that I had been prepared to stand fraudulently in that long suffering queue of pilgrims in order to sneak a glimpse of the oil painting upon which her face had allegedly appeared. Visitation or mass hysterical delusion, I wasn't fussy.

It occurs to me only now, months later, that it wasn't Diana witnesses repeatedly described. Not her, but her picture: 'You know the pose,' said one mourner. 'The picture with her head cupped in her hands. She's got the tiara on as well.' There, floating above Charles I's right shoulder, was an image of Diana that had once been on the cover of Vogue.

Poor woman. Even the Virgin Mary is allowed to shed her iconography when she appears to her faithful. She moves. She speaks. She blesses. She is not confined to plaster statues with imploring hands.

And poor me. More than fifteen years on, I'd still wanted to see the unseeable: a picture coming to life, even after death.

10

I looked at him and thought, it's true, he is the picture of her. I was visiting William at Eton after his mother's death. He was blond, big-toothed and blushing. I decided I liked him, and I knew he was fond of me. What's more, I was concerned that the headmaster's wife would be oh-so-dull. What hope of consolation, I asked myself, can he have with a headmaster's wife?

We were in an old wainscoted room with large leaded windows, and it was warm with September sunlight. I was wearing a black, sleeveless dress. My legs, brown with summer, were stretched out before me, and my bare feet rested on a chair back, though we both knew it was against the rules.

We were very easy together. He told me this was the room where the older boys came for Prep. I winked and told him I knew that, and we laughed with real affection, as if we had stumbled upon a ridiculous pun.

11

At the bus stop the next morning, someone was talking – 'Everyone wants a piece of her.' – and I remembered my dream of William in the night.

12

The paparazzi word for the hunt is 'monstering'. Picture their faces (your face, my face, your Aunt Margaret's face) phantasmagoric* in the reinforced glass of those car windows.

Could it be that she didn't pass over that night? Could she have passed under in the tunnel below the Pont de l'Alma?

Thirteen pillars before the car came to rest. A succession of twelve quick frames: indistinct images of an underworld below the City of Love in which even Orpheus* couldn't resist turning back for a look, draping the dying heroine's arm over Dodi's leg, and snapping a few quick shots.

Twelve frames. Her life flashing before our eyes. Negatives we hold to the thin light of some need, squinting for an absence.

13

*enceinte means pregnant in French
*phantasmagoric is a term used in psychology to describe a 'shifting medley of real or imagined forms, as in a dream' or a technique in films. It comes from a French word meaning production of phantoms or illusions.
*Orpheus: In the Greek myth, the poet Orpheus goes down to the underworld to bring back his wife, Eurydice. He is forbidden to look at her until they reach the earth again, but he turns to see her and loses her forever.

ACTIVITY 37

In groups discuss the story using the following questions as prompts:

- Is the story *about* Diana?
- What expectations did you have of the kind of text you were reading as you read the first section? Did this change?
- What different discourses or styles does the writer draw on in the telling of the story?
- What is the effect of the organisation of the story into thirteen parts?

- What are your views on writing about 'real' characters or drawing on factual material in this way?
- Would you describe this text as a story?
- What do you think this text is saying about the culture of the late twentieth century in Britain?

Now read the commentary, which was written for you by the writer. Then consider the questions that follow.

Story of a Story

On Sunday morning, August 31, 1997, my husband woke me from deep sleep and told me that Diana was dead.

I'm still curious about my own reaction: '*What*?' I breathed. I threw back the covers, ran downstairs, and took up vigil in front of the TV. That groggy morning, the news seemed as unreal as that of a death in the family, and yet, Diana, Princess of Wales, was, clearly, not family.

Nor was she someone to whom I'd given much thought in my day-to-day life. I didn't admire her, particularly. She was interesting, yes, because her life was so ceaselessly documented, yet she had been of no particular interest to me. It is probably the mystery of my own first reaction that morning, so instinctive and urgent, that led me to write 'Dreaming Diana: Twelve Frames'.

On the Monday, the day following her death, I went out and sheepishly bought all the papers. I continued to do so throughout the week, though I wasn't sure why. I knew I'd want to write something about her death at some point – writers, I suppose, are always gathering ideas and watching, even when it isn't necessarily appropriate. I knew the strangeness of my own reaction was not so much mirrored as magnified, endlessly, in the national response to her death; in the outpourings of grief, anger, and loss.

Of course there was genuine tragedy in the story of Diana's death that night in Paris. It was the death of a young woman and mother, and the loss of life, especially that of a parent, is always to be mourned – though, in the vast majority of such cases, it must be said, we do *not* mourn, not as a nation at any rate. There was, too, as some commentators at the time couldn't help but notice, tragedy, 'Greek style', in the circumstances which led to her death. A beautiful princess is driven, almost literally, to death by the very same force which has brought her to fame: the celebration of her image.

The more I thought about it, the more I realised I was interested in the power of – or perhaps, more aptly, the powerlessness of – Diana's image. In her death, as in her life. I wondered if, as mourners, we weren't consumers of her still, possessed by a need to behold her image everywhere. Were we, in reality, mourning Diana, or were we mourning the myriad needs we had, together, projected onto the 'blankness' that was first Diana: a teenage girl who had arrived, unformed, on the scene of our imaginations back in 1980?

Several months after her death, when the public grief had quietened, I dug out that great weight of newspapers and went through the reports of her death and funeral, with the proverbial fine-tooth comb. I was drawn to the small details which were hardly reported at all: the details in a back-page side-column of Diana's post-mortem; the few lines of a dream from an ordinary woman in Manchester; the reports, too brief to be called accounts, of the suicides of two men who had known her largely through her image only; the scattering of wild conspiracy theories.

In all these reports, the image of Diana – in photograph, story or dream – emerged as something to be guarded, hoarded, contained, or controlled. Increasingly, I became interested in the slippery boundary between Diana the Icon and Diana the Commodity. Therein, it seemed to me, lay something like the real tragedy of her death – the fact that, even in our tremendous show of respect for the dead, we still didn't quite know the difference.

Myself included. I couldn't get enough of the coverage through that long TV wake of a week. And my self-knowledge couldn't end there. In an earlier incarnation, at the age of 17, I had been determined to get a picture of Diana when she and Charles visited Halifax, Nova Scotia, where I'd grown up. Not Charles, but Diana. Her appeal had already, in 1983, transcended the fact of her royalty. I knew that this, my own story of Diana – arbitrary and ordinary as any other – would have to frame the story I was about to write. Stories need a sense of the personal, at some level, to give them life. The story being told has to be born of the teller – told for a reason – if it is to grow into more than lively anecdote.

Once I realised this was to be the story of the image of Diana, the form of the story, a series of twelve 'snaps' or 'shots', came to mind very naturally, each shot working as a brief narrative in itself. I wanted to keep each as spare as possible, partly to preserve that sense of a snapshot – of several stories only partially glimpsed – and partly to avoid sentimentality.

I was also struck, as I re-read the papers, by the details of the tunnel under the Pont de l'Alma, where the car in which she was passenger came, finally, to a stop at the thirteenth pillar. I could see, in my mind's eye, the unstoppable passage of the car from the first pillar to the second, from the second to the third, its doomed progress transformed in my mind into a series of slow-motion stills – as impending disasters are so often rendered in film. It seemed important to try to capture, in the very form of the story, that sense of a series of reproduced images: say, twelve seconds' worth of stills or snaps; or the multiple images on a photographer's contact sheet; or the quick and strange succession of dim images you find on a strip of negatives. I wanted to evoke, at once, a sense of the banality (that throw-away quality) of the reproduced image at the end of the twentieth century, and also, a sense of its totemic power in western culture at large, for in Diana's case, the representation of her person had seemingly become more 'real' than she herself was.'

Jean Baudrillard, French sociologist and philosopher, offers an incisive analysis of the rise of the 'simulacrum' in postmodern society – a phenomenon to which Diana, literally, fell prey. A 'simulacrum', we are told by the *Concise Oxford Dictionary*, is an 'image of something; a shadowy likeness, a deceptive substitute, a mere pretence.' Baudrillard develops the idea further. For him, the border between art and reality in contemporary culture has vanished, giving way to the phenomenon of the simulacrum as never before. It's an idea of vital interest and concern to many writers today.

I try to recreate this murky borderland of art/reality in the form of a 'story' which is composed entirely of 'factual' fragments; that is to say, of facts and personal accounts (my own included) which, in turn, echo the dreams, conscious or unconscious, of Diana's many voyeurs. I wanted the story to be multi-perspectival, partly to represent, in fictional terms, the strange collective force that transformed her death into international event; partly to create a sense of a jigsaw of a narrative that can never be entirely completed. Its parts are too many, and they're too contradictory. The more 'real' an event seems to be (e.g. the more televised, reported, photographed, documented), the more I am inclined to explore the 'unreality' which might underlie it. A shifting discourse is one way of doing so. It's less neat; less reassuring.

In his analysis, Baudrillard argues that the simulacrum occurs when the distinction between representation and reality, between 'signs' and what they refer to in the real world, breaks down. He charts this process of breakdown in the following way.*

1) **When an image is first made, it is a reflection of a basic reality.** (Diana, the young nursery nurse, is photographed with children at the school where she works. She is dating Charles, the heir to the throne. She is, therefore, newsworthy.)

2) **In time, the image of the subject comes to mask and pervert a basic reality.** (Diana's face is soon appearing on tankards, tea towels, T-shirts and biscuit tins. What does her image have to do with any of these items? Nothing. The reality of Diana the person is becoming less real than Diana the commodity.)

3) **The image of the subject now marks the *absence* of a basic reality.** (Diana, post divorce, during a trip to the US, headlines the UK national evening news because she is wearing a new hairstyle at a gala function: the 'slicked back' look. Why is this a national headline? What does a new hairstyle say about Diana the person or we, the nation? These questions no longer matter.)

4) **The image of the subject finally bears no relation to reality whatsoever. It is its own pure simulacrum.** (Paparazzi are paid vast amounts for *any* image of Diana. Cameras flash at the scene of her death, where she is only present as an injured body. The week following her death, Diana has never been so absent and, at the same time, so 'reproduced'. A major broadsheet even reports sightings of her ghost, or rather, sightings of the ghost *of her image*, in St. James' Palace, where her body rests.) So, Diana metamorphoses into image without reference. In life, she had been turned into her own shadowy likeness. In 'after-life', she still cannot escape it.

While, as a writer, I do not take the ideas of Baudrillard and 'translate' them into fiction, and while I did not actually refer to or even reflect upon concepts of the simulacrum in the course of writing 'Dreaming Diana', I was aware of them in general terms and, at some level, was interested in all dialogues about image- and icon-making. Good philosophers and theorists, like good novelists and poets, provoke you with questions, and I like to be provoked. No writer can write without an awareness wider than herself – your work gets dull, and you get dull, astonishingly fast. I also like to feel I am taking part in the culture-wide discussion of what makes our times distinctively *ours*, for good or for ill.

Curiosity fuels my writing, and, a sense of curiosity, of *wanting* to know more, is ultimately what I hope to leave my readers. I usually have more faith in questions than in answers. A good story, it seems to me, should not have *a* message or *a* theme. It should always keep at least two balls in the air. Diana: mass commodity or secular icon? Both. And neither. Questions, like noses pressed to windows, take us up close to important possibilities. Left open-ended, a question might also allow reality to remain *more real, more true to itself* because a question preserves, in all its anticipated answers, the innate mutability of the world; its capacity for change.

*For the framework of this analysis, I am indebted to Richard Appignanesi and Chris Garratt, *Postmodernism for Beginners* (Icon, 1995) pp. 130–132.

ACTIVITY 38

Which comments did you find most illuminating in connection with the story?

What does the commentary tell you about the process of writing?

What does it tell you about the writer's engagement with contemporary culture?

Would you describe this text, the commentary itself, as a story?

Do you feel the commentary does justice to the story and your own reading of it?

Do you feel the writer's commentary has a different authority from yours or are they just different interpretations?

Imagine trying to write a Coles Notes type of study guide to this text, using the conventional headings of Plot, Character and Themes. How easy would this be? Do you think such texts should be part of your A level specification?

ACTIVITY 39

You might like to try writing using the ideas you have discussed in this chapter. Take a fairy tale or a myth that you are familiar with, or get hold of a copy of a collection of traditional tales such as Grimm's. Retell the story for a twenty-first century reader. You may wish to write in the style of Carter or Oates. (There is an extract from a student's work on this in Chapter 8.) Alternatively, take a well-known historical event or character and build a new text around them. You might want to work with fragments or you might want to transport your character into a completely different world or type of text and write something fantastic!

In this chapter we have considered writing that can be described as postmodern and examined some examples. Alison MacLeod's short story showed some of the characteristics of texts described as postmodern. It is concerned with modern communications and how our understanding is shaped by media and technologies. It is historiographic and iconographic in that it examines the ways public history is created and icons (worshipped images or people) are made and what they mean to us. It is a hybrid text that makes its meaning by drawing on other texts and invites the reader to be aware of the processes of construction. The story shows us how theory and practice come together explicitly in postmodern texts: it is both a cultural text and engaged in ideas about how cultural texts are produced. This is to use the term 'text' in the broad sense; Princess Diana as an image is a 'text' to be 'read'. However, it would be very much against the spirit of postmodernism to define its characteristics, as among its key ideas are *multiplicity* and *hybridity*: texts that work in many ways and resist simple explanations; texts that are open rather than closed. It is in this spirit that the critic Bakhtin describes the novel as 'in the vanguard of all modern literary development' and regards the continuing excitement and possibilities of prose fiction as 'the zone of maximal contact with the present (with contemporary reality) in all its openendedness'. You might like to discuss whether you agree with this idea from your own reading experience. It certainly seems like a celebratory note on which to end this analysis of fiction.

8 Writing about Prose Fiction

In this chapter you will focus on writing about prose: understanding what you are aiming for as well as looking at examination tasks and real students' work.

Analysing your task

The way that you write about prose will depend upon the contexts of the task. You may write about a novel for coursework, or in the limited time conditions of an examination where you may or may not have the text in front of you. You may be writing about a prose text comparing it to other prose texts of a similar genre or period. You may be writing about previously unseen or pre-released material which you have not studied before. The specifications for AS and A level English vary between the different examination boards, so for each prose text you study you should seek answers to the following questions:

- How will I be assessed on this text? Examination or coursework?
- What length will the work be? (word limit for coursework; time limit for examination)
- What kinds of questions might be set on this text?
- Which of the assessment objectives does this unit attach marks to and how are the marks weighted?

The last question is very important because you need to know if the examiners will be looking for you to show knowledge of texts and genres (AO2); close reading skills (AO3); understanding of different interpretations (AO4) or contexts (AO5). AO1 is your ability to write well about texts. All the tasks you do will require you to hit some, but not necessarily all, of the objectives and more marks may be given to some AOs than others. You would not be doing yourself any favours in an examination to write an answer entirely based on detailed textual analysis (AO3) if the question actually targeted the assessment objectives for context (AO5) and interpretation (AO4).

ACTIVITY 40

Look again at the assessment objectives printed in the box and then at the essay questions that follow. Pick out the key words in each question.

Can you identify which assessment objectives you think the examiners might be particularly looking for?

The Assessment Objectives

AO1	Communicate clearly the knowledge, understanding and insight appropriate to literary study, using appropriate terminology and accurate and coherent written expression.
AO2i	Respond with knowledge and understanding to literary texts of different types and periods.
AO2ii	Respond with knowledge and understanding to literary texts of different types and periods, exploring and commenting on relationships and comparisons between literary texts (only A2).
AO3	Show detailed understanding of the ways in which writers' choices of form, structure and language shape meanings.
AO4	Articulate independent opinions and judgements, informed by different interpretations of literary texts by other readers.
AO5i	Show understanding of the contexts in which literary texts are written and understood.
AO5ii	Evaluate the significance of cultural, historical and other contextual influences on literary texts and study (only A2).

1 With close reference to two or three episodes, discuss the ways in which Shelley makes the novel *Frankenstein* a criticism of the society of her time.
In your answer you should consider the following aspects:
 - portrayal of the family and women
 - the use made in the narrative of particular examples of injustice, inhumanity and abuse of power
 - the importance of money and position.
2 Consider the way Atwood presents Professor Pieixoto's conference speech in The Historical

Notes in *The Handmaid's Tale*. What is its significance in relation to the novel as a whole?
3 Analyse some of the techniques Angela Carter uses to develop her material in the stories in *The Bloody Chamber*. How successful would you say she is in creating something new out of familiar material?
4 By a close study of the passages from *Jane Eyre* by Charlotte Brontë and from *Little Dorrit* by Charles Dickens, compare and contrast some of the ways in which Victorian novelists use landscape to lend resonance to their work.

COMMENTARY All the questions target AO1, which is about communicating your ideas in a clear, well organised style. Question 1 on *Frankenstein* targets all the AOs. The key words that tell you this are: 'close reference' and 'portrayal' (AO3 – close textual analysis); 'the novel' and 'the narrative'(AO2i – knowledge and understanding of genre); 'the ways', 'the use', 'a criticism'(AO4 – interpretations) and 'society of her time' (AO5i – contexts). For question 2 on *The Handmaid's Tale*, the examiner is looking for 'novel as a whole' (AO2); 'presents' (AO3); and 'consider' and 'significance'(AO4 – judgements and interpretations). This is in addition to AO1, but AO5 is not asked for. Question 3 is for an A2 paper and this one targets only AO4 and AO5ii in addition to AO1. The key words are: 'how successful' (AO4) and 'something new out of familiar material', which requires knowledge of the contexts of the writing and of other texts (AO5ii). Also an A2 question, number 4 asks for 'close study' (AO3); 'compare and contrast' (AO2ii) and 'ways in which Victorian novelists. . .' (AO5ii – contexts).

Planning and writing your answer

When you are confident about what the task requires and what the assessment objectives are, then you are ready to plan your answer. It is a good idea to do this in stages. First, 'brainstorm' to gather ideas about the text that are relevant to the question and identify passages from the text or texts that you might use. You then need to order this material by putting the ideas into a sequence. If you are doing a comparative essay, it would be a good idea to plan this in two columns rather than one so that you have ideas and quotations for each point of comparison from both texts. You are then ready to write your introduction. This is a very important part of the essay because a good introduction should answer the question in a summary form. It should give your reader an outline that will be developed in the body of the essay. Think of it as the hanger for the coat. Without it, the coat would be a shapeless mess of material on the floor. Hanging from the coat hanger, the garment's design is clear.

ACTIVITY 41

Look at the following introduction, written by a student in the first weeks of the AS course. Talk together about the paragraph. Try to decide:

- roughly what the question might have been
- what assessment objectives (AOs) the student had been told to target.

Superficially, the story of *'Looking for a Rain God'* appears to be a simple, but disturbing tale of a family's tragedy in a time of drought in a Third world country. However, underneath is a more meaningful story, which questions the tribes people's humanity and character in extreme situations, their moral and religious beliefs as well as the relationships between themselves and that of the dominating, powerful, colonial authorities. This makes it difficult for the reader to appreciate the tale simply for the story itself and to thus draw a simplistic conclusion. When analysing this story and discussing its exploration of power and its effects upon the reader, it is important to consider the historical and political contexts and backgrounds against which the story is set.

COMMENTARY

This is a good introduction because it says something! Introductions that say 'In this essay I am going to look at . . .' often do not address the question or give the reader any idea of what the student thinks. The student had been told he would be marked on AO1, writing a good essay, AO4, offering interpretations and AO5, placing the text in context. You can see how his introduction tells us that the essay will substantially deal with AO4 and AO5. The question that had been set was: 'What does the story *Looking for a Rain God* by Bessie Head have to say about the nature of power and belief?' Here is another student's introduction:

When an age-old nation is suddenly taken over and forced to accept new, alien beliefs and morals, the natives can experience a tragic loss of cultural identity. *'Looking for a Rain God'* is a complex story exploring this loss, and the effects of it on the people and their actions. From one angle it is a direct, seemingly neutral tale of a tragedy befalling those pushed too far by physical suffering, on another, the blame is partially shifted to those who colonised the Africans and caused such forced re-education.

This student, Harriet, has also addressed AO4 but has addressed AO5 (contexts) more implicitly than Jonathan. It is still clear, however, that the essay will place the story in context.

As you write your essay, you should keep reminding yourself of the question and of your introduction, checking, as you start each new paragraph, that you are still 'on the hanger' and your garment has not started to slip off! In each paragraph you should make a point relevant to the title, support this with a quotation or example from the text and then analyse this. Don't let the quote speak for itself, that is your job – it's what you do with it that counts!

Comparing texts

If you are comparing texts, you should ensure you always make meaningful connections and points of contrast. Writing something like 'all these texts are about women' or 'both texts deal with relationships' is almost as vague as saying both texts were published in books or written in English. You need to be very specific when you assemble your points and evidence and as you make your plan. The following example is the introduction and first paragraph written by a student writing a comparative essay in response to the title, 'Compare and contrast the treatment of patriarchy in *The Yellow Wallpaper* and *The Smell*':

Both texts describe a repressive patriarchal society in which expressions and imagination are sidelined. The narrators of both stories are driven mad by the constraints forced upon them, thus the stories use mental illness to expose the 'mad' nature of patriarchy. *The Yellow Wallpaper*, written in the 1890s, depicts a woman's descent into madness because of the restrictions placed upon her by her husband. *The Smell* was written in the 1990s and describes a man who is driven mad by his own rigid regime. The texts, written almost a hundred years apart, one by a woman, the other by a man, treat patriarchy in different ways, but some similarities can be noted, in particular they both self-consciously exploit the conventions of Gothic texts.

Patriarchal lineage is represented by the use of the house. In *The Yellow Wallpaper* the 'hereditary estate' serves as a reminder of historical patrilineal society as well as the place of the narrator's entrapment. This creates an effect often seen in Gothic novels of enclosure and repression. The narrator is physically confined by the 'barred windows' and 'gates that lock' and mentally repressed by a house full of reminders of its 'colonial', imperial and patriarchal past. Similarly, in *The Smell*, all action takes place within the family home, or as the male narrator describes it, 'my property'. 'The wall that surrounds' the property demonstrates the confinement enforced by the 'stern regime' practised within the micro society. This 'regime' is shown to be similar to that of the narrator's 'father's house', therefore presenting us with ideas about inherited oppression. This is similar to the idea of the 'heirs and co-heirs' in *The Yellow Wallpaper*, reminding us of an inherited patrimonial system. In both texts the house represents containment and oppression for the narrator. In *The Yellow Wallpaper*, however, she is trapped against her will, whereas the narrator in *The Smell* uses the house to oppress his family until finally he traps himself up his own chimney. Both texts display the house as having a past and focus on the inheritance of archaic tyrannical forces, typical of the Gothic.

This essay is suitable for A2, where you will have to engage in comparative study of texts. The essay targets AO1, AO4 and AO5ii. The student, Rosie, shows the ability to discuss interpretations and place the texts in historical, social and literary contexts. She makes clear and meaningful connections between them but also highlights their differences and the time that separates their production, which she deals with in more detail later. In comparing the texts, she moves between them in each section of her essay, rather than dealing with one text, followed by the other. Her use of embedded quotation, slotting phrases into her sentences rather than tacking on chunks of text, makes for a fluent style and shows her secure knowledge of the texts.

Preparing previously unseen prose

If you are taking an examination with unfamiliar prose texts, you should go into the examination with a mental checklist of what to look for as you read and annotate the material. Remember you are looking not just at what the text says, but also at how it says it, through language, form and structure. Students tend sometimes to fall back on plot and character when writing about unseen prose, perhaps because the 'marks of the writing' are less obvious than they are with poetry or drama. We have addressed this issue in this book. Also remember that any information you are given on the examination paper or pre-release material about the literary or historical context of the pieces of writing should be taken into full consideration, such as when the text was written or under what circumstances, or what kind of text it is. You may get texts other than fiction, such as biography, criticism, travel writing or letters, for example. In an examination you may find that there are bullet points underneath the question. Remember these are there to help you, but you should treat them as prompts, not as an essay plan in themselves. These prompts will also help you target the AOs.

Recreative writing

You may have the opportunity to undertake a different kind of writing from the formal literature essay. This kind of task still requires close attention to a literary text so that you can reproduce its genre, form and style of language. You will probably also be assessed on a commentary that discusses the relationships between your piece of work and the original text. The following work is by a student who had studied Angela Carter's collection of stories, *The Bloody Chamber*, which we looked at briefly in Chapter 7 of this book. Here is an extract from the end of her own revision of a fairy tale and from the commentary she wrote on how she imitated Carter's prose.

The wolf had curled up on her bed and was in a deep sleep, purring gently. She crept stealthily towards the beast, scooping up the axe that the young man had given her. Just as she raised the axe above the wolf's neck (for even though it had returned her rose it was still a beast and therefore must be killed), the wolf stirred. Frozen with fear, she watched as the wolf's eyes twitched open to reveal the most strikingly beautiful eyes.

They were blue.

It whimpered and reached out its paw tentatively. Against her judgement, and for no plausible reason the Princess followed her instincts and lay down beside the wolf, cradled in its paws.

The next morning the birds were singing and a single beam of sunlight shone on the sleeping bed dwellers. The Princess opened her eyes and was amazed to find the woodcutter's son lying beside her. A beautiful fragrance filled her nose and had the effect of a drug, but she felt in control. She found the source – her single white rose lying in a pool of blood on her bed sheets. The tips of the petals were tinged with red, and the flower had opened:-

In full bloom.

Smiling, she turned back to her young man and returned to slumber.

Extract from Eleanor's commentary:

Carter was interested in Jung's psychoanalytic theory which suggested that mankind is equipped with two distinct and contrasting ways of perceiving: sensation and intuition . . . the Princess shows that she has balanced intuition with her reliance on her senses when 'she followed her instincts and lay down beside the wolf'. She coupled her senses – seeing that the wolf's eyes were 'strikingly blue' with her new found intuition. . . . She 'crept stealthily' and then reverted to her judgement of things by their appearance: 'it was still a beast and therefore must be killed'.

The images of the roses are also in opposition – white is associated with innocence and purity, orange roses are representative of lust and red roses with love. . . . In contrast when it is the fragrance of the white rose she feels in control of her emotions. This is because the smell is of acceptance and freedom from repression. . . In *The Lady of the House of Love*, Carter uses the image of the rose as a motif. The roses echo the sexual awakening of Nosferatu.

I tried to emulate Carter's language by using rich, verbose, Latinate words in long sentences, which feminise the language and engage the imagination. Poetic devices are also used: metaphors, similes and alliterations. 'Echoing emptiness' reinforces the helplessness she feels, and 'single beam of sunlight shone on the sleeping bed dwellers' gives a sense of the feeling of contentment. This use of alliteration can be seen in *The Company of Wolves* where the repetition of the s sounds adds to the tenderness and gentleness being portrayed: 'See! sweet and sound she sleeps'. Carter places lines separately to add to their impact, and often they are motifs. In my story one of the phrases that stands out on its own is the key motif of the rose: 'In full bloom'.

ACTIVITY 42

Imagine you are assessing Eleanor's work. Comment on how successful you feel she is in achieving AO1, AO2ii and AO3 from the section you have read.

In this chapter you have focused particularly on the assessment objectives and how to meet them when you write about prose.

Glossary

All literary terms, terms referring to theoretical approaches and less familiar vocabulary are explained as they are used in the text. The following glossary returns to the technical terms we have encountered in discussing prose fiction, but you should be aiming to extend and build your general vocabulary too, in order to analyse texts precisely.

Bildungsroman A novel about formation or education of a character.

Canon A group of texts given a privileged status in a culture, often referred to as 'classics', but what is in or out of the canon changes over time.

Character A very important convention in the novel, but not always used as 'psychologically' true, so it is important to consider the functions of character and the techniques of characterisation too. Using an alternative term, such as a 'narrative figure' reminds us that they are constructs, not people.

Closure How a text is finished, often how the reader is persuaded to accept an overview or final understanding of a text.

Dialogic A text that offers several voices or world views rather than a single one.

Discourse A way of writing or talking or thinking that is specific to a particular community or ideology.

Epistolary A text told through letters.

Figurative Language that refers to something other than the literal subject, often making comparisons as in similes and metaphors.

Focalisation A third person narration (using *he/she/they* rather than *I*) may be offered through the eyes of a character in the text, the focaliser, acting in a similar way to a camera.

Genre Category or type of text that shares conventions with other texts of the same genre, may be broad, e.g. poetry or more precise, e.g. science fiction, magic realism.

Gothic Texts that share gothic conventions, typically featuring horrific or uncanny events in oppressive settings with tyrants and victims.

Ideology Views on the nature of the world, which may be seen as false and upheld by the sources of power in a culture (which includes texts).

Intertextuality   Relationships between texts. Texts can be meaningful for us because of our reading of other texts.

Magic realism   Texts which bring magical or fantastic elements into otherwise realist narratives.

Metafiction   Texts which play around with the process of writing, drawing attention to their own construction.

Modernism   An early twentieth century literary movement that reacted against the confident techniques of realism.

Narrative   The telling of stories, where it refers to an unfolding sequence of events, which does not only happen in fiction.

Narration   The process of telling of the story by the narrator.

Omniscient narrator   An all-knowing, 'God-like' narrator.

Postcolonial texts   Generally used to describe texts by writers who come from places that were colonised but are now independent.

Postmodernism   Used to describe late twentieth century texts that experiment with form and ask questions about the relationship of texts and the real world – see Chapter 7.

Realism   Writing that sets out to create an illusion of actual people and situations.

Representation   The construction through language of a character or situation, usually the representation of 'reality', which is not of course real.

Rhetoric   The art of persuasion, the devices of language that a speaker or writer uses to convince their audience.

Romance   Stories that deal with events and characters removed from the everyday world, inherited from medieval tales of courtly love.

Speech/dialogue:

Monologue   Continuous speech from one character.

Direct speech/discourse is presented as being actually spoken by using speech marks: *'I really want that one,' he said.*

Indirect speech/discourse   is reported speech: *He said he wanted that one.*

Free indirect speech/discourse in the voice of a character without speech marks: *Just the one, at last! He picked it up.*

Further Reading

You will find there is a great deal of critical material written on the canonical novels, such as those you are studying from the eighteenth, nineteenth and early twentieth centuries.

For more general critical reading on prose fiction:

Malcolm Bradbury, *The Modern British Novel* (Penguin 1994).

This is an interesting, thorough, but quite challenging read that covers the novel from the 1870s to 1990s.

Jeremy Hawthorn, *Studying The Novel: An Introduction* (Arnold, 3rd edition 1997).

Aimed at undergraduates starting to study the novel, but clearly written and with helpful surveys of novels, critical positions and practical advice.

David Lodge, *The Art of Fiction* (Penguin 1992).

Accessible, short essays on all aspects of fiction.

Dennis Walder (Ed), *The Realist Novel* (Routledge 1995).

Very good detailed sections on genre and context. Focuses particularly on *Pride and Prejudice, Frankenstein* and *Great Expectations*. Includes a useful anthology of critical essays.

Fay Weldon, *Letters to Alice* (Cambridge University Press 1998).

Lively 'letters' to a teenage niece about studying Jane Austen but also about fiction writing in general.